PRAISE FOR

DAVID JACKSON AND LANDING AT THE TOP

How many times have we heard someone of great potential express frustration and a sense that they won't be able to accomplish much in life? This aura of pessimism, almost of helplessness, is unfortunately becoming all too common, possibly fueled by a society whose messages are increasingly negative.

Enter *Landing at the Top*, an extraordinary book that shows, by example, how one can, indeed should, set big goals, and how to go about accomplishing them. The stories that the author, David Jackson, shares with us are inspiring, but also fun and exciting. If you ever dreamt of learning how to fly an airplane, but have been afraid to even try, Jackson will guide you through the steps that one needs to take to tackle the most ambitious, and apparently unachievable goals.

This book, that I hope many people will buy, read, and keep as a reference, is a quick read, but it packs a significant amount of practical instruction on how to pursue success. I was truly touched by the heartwarming nature of the stories that fill the book and at the same time impressed because the questions it poses to the reader are exactly what our youth needs, in this time of rapid change, evolving norms, and great uncertainty.

A book that I recommend not only to aspiring leaders, but also to mentors, teachers, parents, and anyone who is ready to set big goals and make them a reality.

– DANIELE STRUPPA
President of Chapman University

For anyone who dreams about being a transformational leader, *Landing at the Top* is a must-read. It not only gives the how-to's of converting dreams into reality, but it also shows how passion trumps obstacles and roadblocks that stand in the way. David Jackson's amazing life is an inspiration for those who want to make a positive difference in the world.

– JIM DOTI
President Emeritus and the Rick Muth Family Chair
in Economics, Chapman University

It has been an honor and a privilege to be employed by Mr. David Jackson for over twenty years. In that capacity, I served under his leadership as an AP Calculus teacher; a position in which he gave me the freedom to dream big, for my students and for myself as an employee of Fairmont Schools. As a result of his unrelenting belief in me and his student population, Mr. Jackson spearheaded one of the most successful AP Calculus programs ever commenced in the entire country. And as such, his school, Fairmont Preparatory Academy was recognized as the Calculus Mecca of the United States for twenty years; literally changing the paradigm as to what was possible and what could be expected if you dared to have a BHAG—Big Hairy Audacious Goals; and you were not afraid to relentlessly chase it, work for it, and accomplish it.

As so clearly demonstrated in his book, and more importantly exemplified by his life, Mr. Jackson has devoted a lifetime to inspiring others to be great and chase their dreams. And, as he would say, "If anyone tells you otherwise—don't listen to them. Just keep reaching for the stars." In this book, *Landing at the Top*, you will be driven to make the world a better place because others like David Jackson believed it was possible; a testament resounded by thousands of students who have graced the halls of Fairmont Preparatory Academy for over a half a century. This book is a must-read for anyone who believes that there are no limits to anything in life if you are just bold enough to pursue it; in short, "Attempt the impossible and you will achieve the improbable."

– SAM "MR. CAL" CALAVITTA

Mathematics, Fairmont Prep Academy; voted Top Calculus Teacher in the World in 2005; eighteen-time triathlete; recipient of the Siemens Award for Advanced Placement; author, *Making a Difference*

David Jackson's *Landing at the Top* is an engaging, inspiring story of a man who dreams bigger than most of us, a man who tackles goals and challenges that might discourage those who lack his boundless determination and optimism. Jackson's myriad accomplishments are impressive, indeed. Equally memorable is the honesty and humility of the man behind the accomplishments. Few authors of his stature so freely acknowledge weaknesses, admit failures, and generously credit those who helped them along the way. In this way, the book serves as much as a how-to, motivational manual as a memoir of a life well lived. Jackson generously shares his "Golden Rules to Live By" and repeatedly cheers us on to a more expansive life with, "If someone like me can have these successes, you can too." Read this book and get inspired.

– DAWN THURSTON

Author, *Breathe Life into Your Life Story: How to Write a Story People Will Want to Read*

Throughout *Landing at the Top*, David Jackson delights us with a series of adventures and achievements that begin with dreams and beliefs, but are then mainly driven by doing, adjusting, and persevering. The "doing" parts, for example, what David did to transform Fairmont Schools, are breathtaking, not just in what he sought to achieve but also how he went about it. Unorthodox to say the least!

Educators, students, and aspiring leaders, take note … sometimes ambitious common sense trumps commonly accepted professional practices! This is much more than a "guy follows his dreams" book. Jackson dreams "smart" as well as "big." I highly recommend *Landing at the Top* for anyone who dreams of making a difference in their schools, work or businesses, and even for your family.

– GUILBERT C. HENTSCHKE

Dean Emeritus, Rossier School of Education,
University of Southern California

In his memoir, *Landing at the Top*, David Jackson chronicles his life filled with overcoming challenges and proving naysayers wrong. His incredible life story recounts the tale of a man who transforms personal setbacks and professional obstacles into a life of "dream achievement"—a life that shaped and impacted thousands of young lives as the leader of a prestigious private school in Orange County, California. His inspirational story of enduring positivity and abundant perseverance will serve to energize and encourage you to always pursue your dreams. This motivational work will provide enduring resolve for young adults to view setbacks as opportunities and will be a source of continued tenacity for those with big obstacles, but even bigger dreams.

– DR. STEVEN SHERMAN
Head of School, Palm Valley School

David Jackson's *Landing at the Top* is an exceptional story that inspires you to reach your big, hairy, audacious goals. It captures the reality of the "ups and downs" of life in regards to reaching success. David Jackson's trials prove that the struggles of life can become your greatest strengths, instead of weaknesses. As a twenty-year-old who is just beginning his journey of setting big, hairy, audacious goals, this biography serves as an inspiring reminder that setting goals leads to the realization that anything is achievable. As you embark into the world of accomplishing your goals, allow David Jackson's life to be an example to you that there is nothing anyone can say or do to diminish your potential.

– DYLAN BARAJAS

We are truly limited by our imagination, and the content of our successes is only limited by our attitudes and actions. Dave Jackson's *Landing at the Top* is a great aid to maximizing what can be accomplished in one's own life.

– RONALD STEIN, PE

Founder of PTS Advance, author, columnist,
Energy Literacy Consultant, and co-author of the Pulitzer Prize–nominated book *Clean Energy Exploitations*

Landing at the Top is a must-read book for the aspiring entrepreneurs and dreamers of the world. David Jackson captures the true essence of leadership as he takes you on his journey, both personally and professionally, with optimism and courage. His valuable insights, passion, and willingness to never accept the status quo, is a true testament to his success as a servant leader. As his colleague, I have observed in awe as he grew his business by setting ambitious standards of excellence for himself and his team. David's tenacity to overcome obstacles without losing heart is truly inspiring. I am grateful he has shared his story with us.

– SHERRY ADAMS

Co-founder, Stratford School, and Vice Chairwoman,
Spring Education Group

This book is more than an autobiography; it's a life guide that illustrates the transformative power of resilience, belief, and audacity in the face of adversity. Jackson's personal journey, from overcoming significant challenges to becoming a leader in education, serves as a testament to the idea that anyone can transcend their limitations. His stories of personal and professional triumphs, underscored by the pivotal role of a sixth-grade teacher who believed in him, highlight the importance of support and belief in unlocking potential. It is this same support and belief he cultivated at Fairmont, where I studied from preschool through high school, that I still use today as a practicing physician. This book highlights remarkable achievements and challenges, as well as showcases the profound impact on students' lives, including mine, that Jackson has had. This narrative doesn't just recount events; it encourages readers to chase their dreams, embrace failure, and persist despite obstacles. It's a compelling call to action for dreamers and doers alike, offering practical wisdom for anyone looking to make an indelible impact in their personal and professional lives. An essential read for aspiring changemakers.

—RANI BERRY, MD

Gastroenterologist

My first tour of David Jackson's Fairmont Private Schools campus confirmed most, if not all, of my first impressions of this man. Purpose driven, tenacity and an unwavering commitment to positively make a difference in young people's lives which would ultimately improve our world. Over the next twenty-plus years, I learned that he was a man with big dreams and where others might ask "Why?" David would ask "Why not?" In his book *Landing at the Top*, Jackson shows us by example how we too can not only reach for the stars, but snatch them on our way to living our best life!

—JACK DALY

CEO coach and world-recognized serial entrepreneur

Mr. David Jackson, you have lived a very productive and successful life. Your life was full of adventures, interesting events, successful contracts, and actions. Your book of memoirs will inspire young people to have concrete aims in their future life.

David Jackson's book, *Landing at the Top* is a very interesting and unordinary story of a man, who reached his dreams in life. It is a special story which can teach us how to set up small aims to reach a bigger goal. The book is like a manual that gives helpful advice on how, through different accomplishments and actions in life, our dreams can come true.

I am sure you *must* read *Landing at the Top*, and you will get inspiration to do something new and good in your life.

– MIKHEIL ELIZBARASHVILI

Chairman, Association Diabetikon

LANDING AT THE TOP

DAVID JACKSON

LANDING AT THE TOP

HOW EMBRACING ADVENTURE CAN LEAD TO EXTRAORDINARY SUCCESS

Advantage | Books

Published by Advantage Books, Charleston, South Carolina.
An imprint of Advantage Media.

Printed in the United States of America.

10 9 8 7 6 5 4 3 2 1

ISBN: 978-1-64225-930-8 (Hardcover)
ISBN: 978-1-64225-929-2 (eBook)

Library of Congress Control Number: 2024907678

Cover and layout design by Matthew Morse.

THIS BOOK IS DEDICATED TO:

My dad, Ken Holt, for inspiring, teaching, and mentoring me.

My mom, Helen Holt, for believing in me and guiding me like a loving friend.

My friend and stake president, Major General Lou Alder.

Stacey, my wife of over fifty-two years, for making my life worth living.
We are sealed for time and eternity by a very loving God.

My five living children and thirteen grandchildren, who never fail to amaze me
and who I am confident will continue to promote our Jackson legacy
of knowing that when you reach that BHAG dream,
the real joy comes from sharing God's gifts with others!

And especially my Heavenly Father, His Son, Jesus Christ, and the Holy Ghost,
who have given me everything I've required, specifically the inspiration
and promptings when I needed them most in life and in writing this book.

CONTENTS

ACKNOWLEDGMENTS 1
INTRODUCTION 3

ONE
A SUCCESSFUL LANDING AFTER A ROUGH TAKEOFF 7

TWO
NEVER GIVE UP 23

THREE
A MUCH-NEEDED HAND IN THE DESERT 33

FOUR
BIG DECISIONS 59

FIVE
BACK IN THE USSR 75

SIX
TAKING OFF 99

SEVEN
SHE SAID YES! 113

EIGHT
SCHOOL SHOULD BE FUN AND CHALLENGING 129

NINE
LANDING AT THE TOP 145

CONCLUSION 183

ACKNOWLEDGMENTS

My heartfelt thanks go out to:

Those who helped inspire me to put this book together: Dawna Thurston and Jack Daly, and Katharine Schroeder at Advantage | Forbes Books, who helped me write it.

Alan Langford, Adrian Arambul, Vlad Zhadkov, as well as Lauren Steffes and Matthew Morse at Advantage | Forbes Books.

My sixth-grade teacher, Mr. Frodshime, who completely turned my life around and made most of my future possible. He believed in me when I didn't believe in myself.

Mr. Ritchie, who gave me my first job in the aircraft industry and helped me learn to fly, and Steve Gibbs, my flight instructor who taught, encouraged, and inspired me to fly.

So many who inspired, encouraged, and pushed me when I needed it and showed me by example. There are too many to list, but I want to try to acknowledge as many as I can; please forgive me if I left your name out!

President Flake, Bishop Henderson, Bishop Dick Haymond, Bishop and Terresa Bell, Bishop and Joan Thacker, Terry Tomlinson, Art Francis, and Todd Remington. My mission partners President and Sister Harrison, Ruth and Steve Littlefield, Dmitry Mikulin, Elder Jörg Klebingat, Bob Greene, Dennis Hardin, Ted Nelson, Sam and Anne Olson, and Paula Burton. Old friends Bob Stires, Bob King, Stuart Frances, Etsaro Nagahisa, Wes Hoover, Bud Paine, Shelagh Williams, Jim Neilsen, Ross Newlin, and David Coombs.

The talented and extraordinary teachers and staff of Fairmont Schools, including Hilda Hosmer, Tom Healey, Rodger Cunningham, Courtney Harritt, Bruce Hockman, Adela Stella, Sam Calavitta, Janet Hall-Molina, Steve Sherman, Lynne Anderson, Carol Calabria, Joedy Gardner, and Steven Whitlock, and so many more.

Lanhee Chen, Rani Berry, Samantha Clement, and all our Fairmont graduates.

Ron Stein, Seth Bass, Austin Hoover, Steve Samuelian, Doug Schaaf, Ron Hoefer, and former Anaheim mayors John Seymour, Fred Hunter, and Tom Tait.

Dr. Jim Doty, Howard Wang, Guilbert "Gib" C. Hentschke, Lance Izumi PRI, Anita Lonstein, Peter Lavaroni, Jerry Luden, Marian Osgood, Gary Stokoe, Nancy Watson, Susan Kline, and Randy Einem.

INTRODUCTION

Are your dreams alive and kicking? Have you set goals for your life? I'm not talking about everyday goals; I'm talking about Big Hairy Audacious Goals (BHAGs).[1] If your dreams and goals don't excite you and make the blood run faster through your veins, may I ask you why not?

Could it be that you've learned to put aside your dreams because a few well-intentioned friends have discouraged you? Have you heard comments such as "You can't do that, you're too young, too poor, too old, too inexperienced"? Have people told you that you're not smart enough or not trustworthy? Throughout my life I've heard all of these remarks—and more—so I hope my stories will help you learn to follow your dreams, never give up, and always try, even if it seems impossible.

Nothing in the world should prevent you from dreaming big and setting enormous, whopping goals. After all, they're your dreams and goals and because of that, no one has the right to tell you that they're ridiculous, unattainable, or unrealistic. Take it from me—just

---

1 Jim Collins, "BHAG, Jim Collins - Concepts," accessed February 12, 2024, https://www.jimcollins.com/concepts/bhag.html.

an ordinary guy who always had a multitude of BHAGs running through his head—the things you can accomplish in your life are only limited by a reluctance to accept that anything is possible if you really want it and you believe in yourself.

Growing up wasn't easy for me, and I suffered from self-doubt caused by emotional and physical challenges that skewed my perception of life. I was born with double vision, and as a young child, I couldn't understand why the letters on a page swirled around, making it impossible for me to learn to read. In 1951, I contracted encephalitis and meningitis and lived in a world that was under the constant threat of polio. Because of my vision problems and frail health, my academic journey became a monumental struggle. I was mocked by my peers, dismissed by my teachers, and on a path to surefire failure until I was saved by a sixth-grade teacher named Mr. Frodshime.

Mr. Frodshime was a World War II veteran who had, as he put it, "an encounter with a grenade that didn't go well." He lost his left arm and three fingers on his right hand, but never let that limit his capacity to inspire and motivate others. He saw something in me that no one—especially me—had ever seen before. He saw potential. In class, he challenged me and pushed me, never letting me get away with anything and refusing to accept excuses. He helped me discover the strength within myself to overcome obstacles; he believed in me and taught me to believe in myself. My experiences in Mr. Frodshime's classroom would end up having a profound effect on my future in so many ways, including influencing me years later in my career as an education entrepreneur.

There were many other agonizing events during my childhood, including a terrible accident when I was three years old that almost killed me and left both my parents with severe injuries. I suffered from terrifying nightmares when I was only seven, and at age thirteen, I had my heart broken and experienced a lot of anger when my parents divorced. But it was in all these trials I faced that I discovered resilience and realized that even the worst experiences can lead to profound moments of growth. This did not happen overnight; these discoveries and realizations have continued throughout my life. I recognized that the audacious dreams I had—and would continue to have over the years—could be accomplished *because* of the obstacles I faced and not *despite* them.

I think about my goals in life as mountain peaks to summit, and as I stand now at the top of the mountain and look down, I know that despite how difficult many of the climbs were, despite the occasional slip or fall, they've all been worth it. I've experienced things in my life that I never would have thought possible: the exhilaration of racing against the world's best skiers, the adrenaline rush of piloting a fighter jet, and the thrill of discovering the awe-inspiring beauty of seven continents. I've known the warmth of a large and loving family and the joy of spiritual fulfillment. I've taken pride in owning and running one of the most successful education businesses in the country and experienced the thrill of seeing my students reach beyond what they thought possible to find success in the world's top universities and companies. I've delighted in watching the joy they find in their dream vocations and the happiness they experience raising successful families.

I share my journey with you, not as a mere recounting of events but as a call to action. Don't let life's stumbling blocks hinder you from pursuing your dreams. Don't surrender to the naysayers. Embrace failure as another valuable lesson learned, for each stumble and each mistake brings you closer to success. It's not easy, I will tell you. It can be very hard! Take that leap of faith, take that risk, and reach for the stars, because in doing so, you're not just dreaming, you're living. You can live your dream!

You see, I was once the "dumb kid" who disliked school yet I ended up spending the better part of my life shaping young minds as the head of a prestigious private school. If an ordinary person like me, someone with some extraordinary challenges, can scale the walls of impossibility, so can you. So, let's embark on this journey together; let me share my experiences and help you discover your own determination and resilience to achieve all of your BHAGs.

Are you ready?

1

A SUCCESSFUL LANDING AFTER A ROUGH TAKEOFF

August 11, 1962: In the skies above the desolate landscape surrounding Las Vegas, Nevada. My heart was pounding in my chest, and the adrenaline was racing through my veins.

The plane I learned to fly in

"Mayday! Mayday! This is Cessna 7149 Tango requesting an emergency landing," I yelled, remembering to use my best aviation vernacular despite my panic.

"7149 Tango, Las Vegas Tower. What is your emergency?" came the swift reply.

I couldn't believe my inaugural solo cross-country flight had transformed into this nightmare. I'd embarked from Fullerton, California, aiming for the stars, and I thought I was well aware of the realities of this flight. Now I worried that I may have made a mistake when I convinced my flight instructor, Steve Gibbs, to let me do an eight-hundred-mile flight through the Nevada and Arizona deserts. Normally, a pilot's first solo cross-country flight should span only fifty nautical miles and just one other airport. He felt this might be too much for me and worried that I wasn't ready for such a monumental test of courage, resolve, and aptitude. I could only hope he was wrong.

Recently I'd run into an old timer who had complimented me on taking on such an audacious adventure at the tender age of sixteen, and his words had fueled my resolve to succeed. I was soaring on cloud nine, blissfully unaware of what was about to happen. Maybe his praise added a little too much to my cockiness about being a pilot?

After the first leg of the flight, I landed safely at the airport in Las Vegas to refuel. I'd done everything my flight instructor had taught me, checking the oil and doing a careful walk-around, then starting up the engine. My confidence was high, and I was ready for the next stage of my flight. Just as I took off, my exhilaration turned to sheer terror. The door of the plane's cowling, that stubborn metallic shield guarding the engine, had come unhinged, threatening to plunge through my windshield. The alarming noise it made and the horrifying sight of it flapping wildly sent chills down my spine. I was sure it was going to rip through my windshield.

"Las Vegas Tower, 4-9er Tango, the cowling door has busted open. I am on my first solo cross-country flight, and I'm sixteen years old."

I was swiftly approaching hysteria and knew I had to get a grip on myself and concentrate. I heard Steve's voice in my head: "Stay in control and don't panic." Every emergency scenario he'd put me through during my initial flight training played in my mind like a movie. I imagined Steve saying, "All right. Stay calm. What are you going to do?"

Taking a deep breath, I steadied my hands on the yoke. "You can do this," I told myself. "Maintain speed. Plan your approach, no sharp turns, make sure your seatbelt is snug, prepare to turn off the fuel after touching down …"

"4-9er Tango, Las Vegas Tower. Can you safely make a 180-degree turn and land on runway 24?"

"4-9er Tango, affirmative."

"4-9er Tango, Las Vegas Tower. Maintain your speed, turn right, and enter downwind for runway 24. I will divert the other traffic and clear you for an emergency landing. We are alerting Airport Rescue and Firefighting to prepare for your landing."

"49 Tango, roger."

"4-9er Tango, Las Vegas Tower. You are cleared for an emergency landing on runway 24. I'll help guide you to a safe landing. Don't worry, you'll be all right."

I wanted to scream out, "That's easy for you to say! You aren't sixteen years old and all alone inside a broken airplane!" Instead, I followed his instructions and miraculously landed the airplane. The relief I felt as my tires kissed the runway was immeasurable.

When I'd begun planning the trip Steve had recommended a safer local cross-country flight. But I was sixteen and craving an audacious journey. I wasn't in the habit of standing up to Steve, who was only twenty-two at the time but seemed much older and wiser. He was larger than life and highly confident. He reminded me of the Marlboro Man, and he was my hero. I held firm and finally he gave in and told me that I would be OK if I remembered all the emergency procedures he'd taught me. His confidence in my abilities gave me the courage and determination to follow my dream of flying cross-country.

After this traumatic experience, I entertained thoughts of staying the night in Las Vegas, catching an Elvis show, and having a relaxing evening. My thoughts went back to Steve, who I knew would never abandon a flight because of a minor emergency. So, I put dreams of Elvis tickets aside, snapped back to reality, and got ready to continue to Phoenix. As I flew across the Nevada and Arizona deserts, I got my confidence back and was enjoying a smooth journey when catastrophe struck again! As I approached the airport in Phoenix, I hit a bird. I couldn't believe it. "Here we go again," I said to no one.

Wow, I hit a bird!

"Phoenix Tower!" I cried out. "Cessna 7149 Tango requests an emergency landing! I just hit a bird!"

"49 Tango, Phoenix Tower. What size bird? Are you able to make the runway?"

"Phoenix Tower, 49 Tango. It was a fairly large bird," I said, although I had barely seen it. All I could focus on was the big dent in my left wing.

"I'm a student pilot on my first solo cross-country," I said with a little more urgency in my voice while thinking that this couldn't be happening again.

Despite the tension, I went through my self-reassurances as I approached the runway. "Stay calm. Stay focused. Stay in control." Finally, I heard the sweet squeal of tires hitting the runway of Phoenix Airport and knew I was safe. After refueling and being reassured that my wing would not fall off, I continued on my journey. The flight back to Fullerton was uneventful and my stepdad was surprisingly understanding about all the damage I'd done to his plane.

You might wonder why I continued flying that day. The answer is simple: I could not let fear change my life goals and plans. For me, this flight was more than a journey toward receiving my pilot's license. It was a voyage of self-discovery, a quest that proved to me I could overcome any obstacles thrown in my path, even birds and broken cowlings! Each emergency landing brought me closer to myself and taught me invaluable life lessons. I was learning that life, like that solo flight, is a journey filled with unexpected turbulence. We have to have courage, maintain focus, and adapt to change as we go along. That maiden solo cross-country flight began shaping the man I am today.

That sixteen-year-old novice pilot has been replaced by a resilient man, a lifelong student of the skies, who not only survived his first flight but emerged victorious. And while life continued to be a series of hurdles, I learned to jump them, for I knew that each obstacle was put there to help me understand myself and my journey. For those of you just embarking on your journey, remember to always pack your courage. Stay firm in your resolve, and even if you're faced with a busted cowling door or an unexpected bird strike, know that you can land safely. Just like that sixteen-year-old did all those years ago above the Nevada and Arizona deserts.

At this point, you've heard the story about my sixteen-year-old self taming the beast that was my first solo flight. You may be wondering how a teenager making a dollar an hour ever got a pilot's license on his own without financial help. Let me share how I did it.

Susan, Mom, Bob, Dad, and me

It began when my mom married Mr. Ken Holt, my boss at the time and owner and head of Fairmont Schools where my younger brother studied. My mom and dad had divorced in June 1958, and

Mr. Holt and his ex-wife Edna had divorced several months before that. I was very upset at the time, but slowly got over it. My sister and I had been hired to work at Fairmont in the summer of 1959 as summer camp junior counselors. My entire life changed when Ken became my stepfather in November 1959.

Shortly after Ken and my mom married, he introduced our whole family to skiing, which we will talk more about later, and when I turned fifteen, he took me flying in his private airplane. It was the first time I'd ever been in an airplane, and it was thrilling! I was awestruck that everything on the ground looked like toys—houses, cars, people. It was a world made of toys. I loved the adrenaline rush during takeoffs and landings. I was hooked and I decided right then and there that I wanted to be a pilot.

However, there was a challenge. How could a sixteen-year-old gas station worker, earning a dollar an hour, afford to obtain a pilot's license? I turned to my stepfather for guidance but his responses to my questions weren't what I was expecting. Instead, he posed questions that sparked my curiosity and drove me to seek the answers myself.

Me: I loved flying with you and now I'm hooked. How do I get a pilot's license?

Ken: How can you find out?

Me: I don't know, I never talked to anyone who has a pilot's license except you.

Ken: How badly do you want to be a pilot?

Me: Real bad of course. I really want to be a pilot!

Ken: How are you going to find out what it takes?

Me: I guess I could go to an airport and talk to some of the people there and find out what it takes.

Ken: Sounds like a good idea. When are you going to do that?

Me: I'll go tomorrow after school and before work. I really want to find a way to get my pilot's license.

As you can see from this exchange, Ken never gave me the answers, but instead inspired me to go find the answers myself.

I began my research and found out that it cost a lot more to get a pilot's license than I ever thought it would. Realizing how long it would take me to make enough money to pay for lessons, I became depressed and decided to talk to Ken again.

Me: I went to the airport, and I don't see how I'm going to ever get my pilot's license!

Ken: So, do you know how much it will cost?

Me: Yes, about $600, not including taxes and the money I'll need for gas and insurance for my car—I don't see how I can do it. Even if I work for two or three years I can never make that much.

Ken: Are you sure? How badly do you want to fly?

Me: Very badly! Can you help me?

Ken: That's what I'm trying to do now. How can you find out if there is a way to get it cheaper?

Me: I guess I could get another job during the summer and talk to the flight school people about what I could do to get a break in the cost.

Ken: Sounds like a good start. What else?

Me: I guess I could see if I could get a job at the airport. Then it wouldn't take so long to get from work to my lessons.

Ken: So, when are you going to do that?

Me: Tomorrow morning.

After this and subsequent conversations, I realized that I had originally expected and wanted Mr. Holt to tell me how to get a pilot's license and even help pay for it. However, I learned that Ken was showing me a path rather than leading me on one. He was encouraging me to find my way and teaching me the value of self-reliance. I soon learned that a lesson was more precious than any amount of money he might have offered. It wasn't until many years later that I realized what a great lesson he taught me about parenting, another one worth its weight in gold.

I succeeded in getting a job at the airport, but it was the unglamorous task of pulling weeds on the tarmac (the blacktop area at an airport). It was terrible! Sometimes it got up to one hundred degrees and more. I hated it, but each time when I got home and complained to Ken, he would calmly ask me, "How badly do you want to learn to fly?" Sometimes I felt angry, but I knew he was right, so I stuck it out for two full weeks. My boss, Mr. Ritchie, was so impressed that I kept coming back and working so hard that he gave me a new job working with the aircraft refueling driver to gas and service aircraft on the field. I was overjoyed! It was a great job that came with a raise and a 25 percent discount on all ground school and flight lessons, fuel, books, and flight supplies. And no more pulling weeds on the hot tarmac.

I then discovered another great benefit that would save me a lot more money and time. Mr. Ritchie would occasionally let me join him on a flight to Las Vegas, San Diego, or San Francisco to pick up clients. I got free instruction one way and I could do my homework on the way back. It was fantastic.

Just a year later, I received my private pilot license. I think I was the first student at Anaheim High School to have a pilot's license, and I was proud of it. During this time, I watched the movie *Jet Pilot* with John Wayne and immediately decided that I wanted to be a fighter pilot for the Air Force, Navy, Marines, or whoever would take me. I know you may be wondering why someone who was born with double vision and had a poor health history would have such lofty aspirations, but that didn't bother me at all. I'd had two eye surgeries that corrected my double vision, so why wouldn't the military want me to fly a fighter? I could not give up and I had to at least try.

I did try, but as you probably guessed, I was rejected with a 1Y draft rating, which meant I'd never be a fighter pilot. But I couldn't just give up! And I didn't give up. A few years later I worked hard and received my aircraft instrument rating. I was on the way to reaching what I now refer to as a BHAG. If I couldn't become a military fighter pilot, then I could eventually own and fly my own jet.

Over the next fifty years, I flew whenever I could and had many exciting and sometimes scary experiences, a few of which I will share later in this book. My policy of never giving up on a dream would one day pay off. It would take five decades, but after serving two separate missions to Russia for my church—a total of three and a half years—with my wife Stacey, I learned that I could qualify to fly a Russian MiG-29 fighter jet from a Russian military base in Siberia. I planned to finally reach my BHAG and have my adventure in October of 2008. Unfortunately, another one of those obstacles or seemingly impossible hurdles got in my way again, and we ended up being blacklisted out of Russia in February 2008. It would take us seven long years to recover from that very difficult and challenging mission. (More about that later.) We didn't volunteer to serve in Russia again until 2015.

We were scheduled to end our mission and fly home in late October 2016 so I booked my MiG-29 flight for August 2016 to avoid the frigid cold expected in October in Russia. Incredibly, my resolve to fulfill my dream of being a fighter pilot was again tested in June 2016 when I had the worst skiing accident in my then fifty-seven-year life of skiing, this time in a huge indoor Moscow ski hill. I broke my right femur, the biggest and strongest bone in your body.

It was the worst experience I have ever had, and I thought it would finally end my BHAG to fly a MiG-29 fighter jet.

I was devastated, but I did not give up hope. I didn't cancel my flight but asked to postpone it until October 6, just before we were to depart for home at the end of our eighteen-month mission. I had to work very hard with the rehab, but I was determined to do all I could to be able to fly that MiG. They said I had to be able to walk completely on my own without any aids. It worked, and although it was painful, it was well worth it!

On October 6, 2016, I fulfilled my dream of flying that MiG fighter jet over Siberian airspace for forty-five minutes. It was one of the most memorable and exciting experiences of my life!

Me in MiG-29 at 58,000 feet

That flight and the solo cross-country flight I took as a sixteen-year-old were just a few of the many experiences I've had that have taught me perseverance and the importance of trusting myself. Some of the things I've done in my life that I will discuss in the next chapters have been exciting, some scary, some painful. But through them all there are common themes that I hope you will embrace and make part of your mindset. You can reach your goals and even achieve those BHAGs if you follow a few of my tried-and-true rules.

DAVID'S GOLDEN RULES TO LIVE BY FOR ACHIEVING YOUR DREAMS

- Believe in yourself and try.
- If you don't ask, the answer is always no.
- Have faith and follow your heart.
- Persistence pays. Don't give up.
- There is value in setting goals and working hard.
- Always do your best and always do the right thing.
- Don't listen to people who tell you that you can't.
- Take advantage of every single righteous opportunity that comes along.
- Have ingenuity. Be clever, inventive, and resourceful.
- Ask God. He will help, especially if your life is based on truth, integrity, and honesty!

I mention God in my list, but this book is for people of all faiths or those with no faith. I can't say it doesn't matter what your beliefs are, but even if you don't have spiritual belief, you must believe in yourself. I didn't have much of a spiritual connection in my early years, but later in life, I made that connection, and my faith has continued to strengthen. Faith has helped me lead with my wife and family, and it empowered us to overcome some experiences that would have otherwise broken us, including the loss of several of our children. But that's my experience.

I truly believe you can follow your dreams and reach your goals through faith, perseverance, and the support of extraordinary people who will guide and believe in you. Remember, I was not born with any great talents or gifts and wasn't raised in a religious household. I was just an ordinary kid with double vision who hated school, caught a very dangerous disease as a young child, and didn't have many friends. Did that little kid think for a minute that he'd have a rewarding forty-four-year career running a prestigious private school in California? No way!

My MiG-29 takeoff

Did he ever imagine he'd fly a fighter jet or ski with Olympians? YES! But the odds against it seemed insurmountable and it appeared everything and everyone opposed it! But I did all those things because I set monumental goals (remember the BHAGs), learned to believe in myself, and embraced all the principles that I listed above. And you can too.

THE FUN SIDE OF FLYING

Ask any young pilot just starting out and they'll tell you that flying an airplane is an exhilarating experience. Of course, this was true for me, but what was even more fun was pulling some simple stunts to scare my friends—and sometimes their parents—when I was piloting for them. Remember, I was a teenager! One of the funniest pranks I'd play was to maneuver the plane to cause a moment of weightlessness. It's not a dangerous thing to do; you just pull the airplane up a bit and then push down hard. It causes that same sensation you get when you go down a steep hill on a roller coaster and you're briefly lifted out of your seat. Most of my friends loved it, although there were a few who didn't appreciate my antics.

Sometimes I'd pull out the cigarette lighter just as we achieved weightlessness and let it go floating in the cabin. I'd pretend that an important piece of equipment had broken free, screaming, "Oh no! What happened? What am I going to do?" This particular stunt did not sit well with the father of one of my friends, who nearly banned his son from ever flying with me again.

Catalina Airfield on top of Santa Catalina Island, CA

When I flew jaunts to Catalina Island, I'd take advantage of the fact that the airport runway was built on a mountain, and there were sheer drop-offs on either end. After takeoff, instead of climbing out, I would fly about fifteen feet over the runway as I built up speed and then just as the runway ended, instead of pulling up, I'd push the plane down.

If I was really being a jerk, I'd scream, "Oh no! Oh no! We're going to crash!"

Some of my passengers got pretty angry, but most of the time they'd forgive me because I'd swoop down and show them a herd of buffalo that lived on the island, and they thought that was pretty cool.

I also had some fun adventures with Steve, my flight instructor. Once, after takeoff at Bishop Airport, instead of climbing to our proper altitude, Steve asked if I would like to fly low and follow the Owens River down the valley before it reaches the Tinemaha Reservoir, where it is diverted into the LA Aqueduct. I thought maybe we would follow it at 1,000 feet, which I was taught was the lowest level you could fly over the ground except when landing. Well, Steve took us down to 200 feet, 100 feet, and even 50 feet! It was awesome and exciting, but when I asked him why we could fly below 1,000 feet, he just told me to trust him.

Later, he quoted from the regulation manual: "An aircraft must maintain an altitude of 500 feet above the surface, except over open water or sparsely populated areas. In those cases, the aircraft may not be operated closer than 500 feet to any person, vessel, vehicle, or structure."

That was great with me; I loved the feeling of speed as we flew 120 mph over the river making sharp right and left turns. When he let me fly and turn with the river, I felt like the pilots I'd seen in the movies, engaging in dog fights and strafing missions during World Wars I and II. It was intoxicating!

BHAG GENERATOR

Everyone should learn to dream and make a list of BHAGs. Take the time to write them down and create the steps you will take to achieve them. Then simply DO IT! I will share more stories and "How-To's" in the following chapters.

Start using some of my Golden Rules now and pick the ones you feel most comfortable with first. I suggest making one of them "If you don't ask, the answer is always no!" and don't give up on those BHAGs!

2

NEVER GIVE UP

In chapter 1, I talked about the importance of having big dreams, believing in yourself, and, most importantly, never giving up. I want to add that no matter where you are in life, it's never too soon or too late to dream big and set goals. It doesn't matter if you're a high school student, working at your first job, or finishing up your final job and preparing for retirement. Heck, even if you're already retired, you can still have dreams and goals, even BHAGs!

There's no timeline for dreaming and setting goals, and there's no better time than right now to get started pursuing your greatest life, a life filled with joy and happiness. Even if you never reach the pinnacle of your dreams and goals, you can make the experience a fantastic journey just by trying and not giving up. If you dream big but only realize part of your dream, that's OK because you will experience a sense of accomplishment, joy, and success just by trying.

I hope that the stories and advice I shared in chapter 1 about falling in love with flying and receiving my pilot's license but not reaching my BHAG of becoming a fighter jet pilot will show you that it's the journey that matters more than the actual goal. No, I never became a fighter jet pilot, but fifty years later, I was able to fly a fighter jet and experience the feeling of being one. My point is that you don't have to achieve every goal to have feelings of success and excitement because the pursuit of your goals will give you tremendous joy and satisfaction.

To help kick-start you on your fantastic journey to reach your goals and fulfill your dreams, I will share with you how I got started on another of my BHAGs. It was, some said, a crazy idea fraught with danger and a seemingly impossible goal, but that didn't stop me from overcoming obstacles, barreling through roadblocks, and ignoring the advice of doubting Thomases and well-intentioned but discouraging friends.

Before I tell you about my pursuit of a crazy dream of becoming an Olympic skier, I'd like to share a little of my background with you so you can see that things weren't easy for me when I was growing up, but I never let that stand in the way of dreaming of big adventures and thrilling experiences.

As I mentioned, I struggled with double vision and that had a profound effect on my childhood. The condition was caused by a doctor using forceps a little too vigorously during my birth, injuring my eyes. For those of you who don't know, forceps look like a giant pair of curved tongs and are used to pull a baby out of the birth canal during a difficult delivery. They are rarely used today, but back in the olden days when I was born, their use was much more common. Forceps can cause a lot of damage to a baby including skull fractures, lacerations, and external eye trauma.

In my case, the doctor accidentally caught my eye socket with the forceps, stretching my eye muscle and causing the injury that would affect my vision and prove to be a major source of my childhood suffering. My mom told me that she heard the doctor say "Oops!" during the birth—not a word you want to hear from a doctor—and although I looked as beat up as a boxer after a knockout, she wasn't aware there was any damage.

She would discover this years later when she noticed that I sat really close to the television, looking at it almost sideways. It was the only position that would allow me to see somewhat clearly. She took me to an eye doctor who prescribed specialized exercises that I had to do every day. I hated it so much, and I felt miserable. I endured this for a year before they finally found a surgeon who thought he could fix the problem. After the surgery, I had patches on both my eyes and was told that if I didn't lie on my back, my eyeballs would fall out. (Yes, they used these kinds of scare tactics on kids long ago.)

To this day, I hate sleeping on my back. I remember the flat-out terror I felt during the two weeks I had to lay with patches covering my eyes, worrying that when they took them off, I would be totally blind. As it turned out, I wasn't blind, but I still had double vision since the surgeon had over-corrected my eyes. I ended up having to wait another year to have a second surgery, during which time I was forced to do the horrible exercises every day.

At school, I couldn't learn to read no matter what I did because the words jumped around on the page. There was no outward sign of any problems with my eyes, so the teachers just thought I was slow. They were not the kindest people and did nothing to make me feel anything but dumb and ashamed. It was just awful, and I hated school. Later, my mom told me that I would cry and cry, begging not to have to go to school. To make matters worse, by the time they finally corrected my double vision, they were past teaching basic reading skills in school, so I was always lost and confused. On top of that, my family moved constantly for my dad's work, and until I was in sixth grade, I was never in the same school for more than one year. Every year it was a new school, new kids, and new teachers who knew nothing about my struggles with reading.

School was a never-ending nightmare for me, and I always thought that it was kind of ironic that I ended up devoting the majority of my life to educating children at the Fairmont School. I think that my early experiences at school affected the way I view education, especially early childhood education. I always say that if I could work out a way to have every child go through the Fairmont School system from preschool to at least third grade, I would be setting them on a path that would virtually guarantee success no matter what they did in life. That's how confident I am in the Fairmont Schools, and I know I owe a lot to my own school experience in teaching me how to shape the best program for young learners.

Other traumatic events occurred during my childhood, including a horrific head-on car crash while I was traveling to Wyoming with my family at the age of three. I was thrown through the windshield and landed bruised but not seriously hurt in a field. My mom and dad suffered severe injuries, but miraculously, my sister was unhurt. I don't remember anything of the accident or its aftermath, but I know that I was separated from my parents while they healed and the whole experience was traumatic and terrifying.

All in all, I was a pretty happy and positive kid despite the car accident, the eye problems, and a scary case of encephalitis and meningitis when I was about nine. As I mentioned, my dad's job required us to relocate frequently, so I didn't really form many lasting friendships until sixth grade and junior high school. When I was eleven, I kept busy with my paper route and learned a lot of great business lessons just by delivering papers!

First job as a paper delivery boy for Anaheim Bulletin

I found that if I could throw the paper up to the porch instead of tossing it in the yard or driveway, my customers were appreciative. I learned to speak kindly and professionally to them when collecting their payments, and I ended up receiving a lot of monetary tips. These were valuable lessons to learn at a young age. I think that constantly being put into new situations and meeting new people helped me learn to be more self-sufficient and adaptable.

It wasn't until I was older and we settled in one area that I began to develop lasting friendships. I even started doing better in school thanks to Mr. Frodshime and a couple of high school teachers who showed me how to believe in myself. The pinnacle of my childhood was finally getting better grades than my sister, who was always the "smart one." It finally happened when we were in junior high, and my sister started paying more attention to her social life than her homework. I was learning to believe in myself, and it affected my grades in the best way. My parents were proud of me, and I was proud too! The positive attitude that I worked so hard to embrace would serve me well for many years to come. I can't stress enough how important your attitude is when you're facing the endless challenges life has to offer. It doesn't cost a dime to find the positive in difficult situations, but the payout is big.

During the difficult times of my childhood, I had only my family and myself to rely on to get through. Many people rely on their faith to carry them over the rough spots, but my family was not religious at all. My mom was an inactive member of the Church of Jesus Christ of Latter-day Saints, also called the Mormon Church, and my dad was an inactive Baptist and completely anti-Mormon. To add to the confusion, my mom felt it was important that we attend some kind of services, so she would take us to whatever church was in the neighborhood we happened to be living in at any given time.

My sister had a Catholic friend in Washington State and so we attended Catholic churches, then Protestant churches, and others. My maternal grandfather was a practicing Mormon and was able to convince my father to allow us to be baptized when I was ten years old, but dad would not allow us to go to Mormon Church services. Clearly, this caused some confusion for me as a young child, and I grew up wanting nothing to do with religion. But I was blessed to have loving parents who taught me to be a good and moral person and always encouraged me.

So, let's move on to my story about how I discovered skiing, and later I will tell you how my love of skiing and my desire to be on an Olympic ski team led to a great adventure. I had never thought much about skiing until my mom married Ken Holt in November 1959 when I was fourteen years old. A few weeks after they married, Ken took our newly combined family of five kids (three of my mom's and two of Ken's) for our first Christmas vacation in the mountains where he would introduce us to skiing. I didn't know anything about skiing, but it sounded exciting to me, so I was all in.

We drove to Green Valley Lake in the San Bernardino Mountains, a quaint ski area where they used rope tows and Poma lifts (those discs you sit on that hoist you up a mountain) and was, according to Ken, good for beginners.

After spending the morning helping my younger siblings put their ski boots on and getting a few lessons on how to walk on longboard skis, we were ready to ski. As we approached the rope tow, a weird-looking contraption consisting of a very long rope looped around two old automobile rims and powered by a small automobile engine, I thought to myself, "That doesn't look too hard."

I reached out and grabbed the rope just as I heard my stepdad shout, "Don't grab the rope! Let it slide through your fingers, then squeeze until it starts pulling you up the hill!" But it was too late. I felt a violent jerk as I grabbed the rope, and I thought my arms were being pulled out of their sockets. I flew up like a ragdoll and then—bam! Down I went in a tangled mess as the rope tow pulled me up the hill like a flopping wet noodle.

By the time Ken repeated the instructions I could barely hear him through all the laughter around me and the tow operator screaming for me to let go of the rope. My own brothers and sisters were bent over double laughing as I finally let go, losing my skis and rubbing my burning hands. The indignity of it all! My pride was bruised more than I was, but I felt like the biggest fool.

1959 rope tow

Ken saw the embarrassment and frustration on my face and raced right over saying, "David, don't give up! You can do it. This time slowly squeeze the rope and then grip it like your life depends on it."

I got up, brushed myself off, put my skis back on, and with renewed confidence I gave it another try. I slowly grabbed the rope, squeezed, and off I went. As I was pulled up the hill, I was feeling pretty proud of myself until I realized that I had no idea how to get off when I reached the top! Right then and there I vowed that if I fell again, I would quit skiing for all eternity.

I watched the guy in front of me as he approached the top and noticed that he let go and turned to the right, so I did the same. I wobbled a little, but made it! Now all I had to do was wait for Ken to arrive and show me how to get *down* the mountain. He'd given me some quick lessons on how to snowplow and walk on the skis, but when you're standing at the top of a mountain you're expected to actually ski down, it's a whole different story.

"Follow me!" shouted Ken, as he took off down the hill.

"Wait!" I cried as I pushed myself with the poles to get started. "This isn't as easy as it looked when you showed me at the bottom of the hill!"

Of course, I fell down. I ended up lying on my side, completely unable to get up. After a monumental struggle, I was back on my feet and noticed my sister Susan doing the snowplow, so I tried that. By this time Ken was halfway down the mountain, and I was snowplowing and falling, snowplowing and falling. It took me over an hour to get down the hill, and by the time I did, I was angry at Ken and at myself. I was ready to quit this ridiculous sport, but Ken was right there to reassure me and encourage me not to give up. So, the next day I reluctantly went with the rest of my family back to the ski area to try again. After several falls and some success, I was zipping down the mountain and loving every minute of it!

I practiced every day and by the end of the week, I was taking on steeper, longer slopes. I had fallen head over heels in love with skiing, and it would become the main focus of my life for the next ten years. Our parents got us involved in the Southern California Junior Ski Racers and we were off every weekend during winter training and ski racing throughout California. My mind was on skiing every waking minute, and I decided that I wanted to train to become an Olympic skier. I can't help thinking that if Ken hadn't encouraged me that first day on the slope, I might have given up right then and there and never known the joy that skiing brought to my life. It also set me off on one of the greatest, most dangerous, and most memorable adventures of my life.

BHAG GENERATOR

The time to get started on realizing your dreams and goals is now. Don't wait until tomorrow or the next day or the next year. Take a moment to think about a time when you abandoned a dream or goal because it was too difficult. Write it down and then write down some ideas of what you could have done differently to achieve the dream or goal.

Start dreaming now, and write down all the exciting, crazy, and fun ideas you have heard about but probably never thought you could do. Then start researching each of them until you know if one of them is worth the work it would take, and don't let anyone try to convince you that it's impossible or ridiculous!

3

A MUCH-NEEDED HAND IN THE DESERT

At the start of the last chapter, I mentioned that regardless of what point you're at in your life, if you want something badly enough, you should go for it. I believe this wholeheartedly and encourage you to believe it as well. But some of you might think that it's easier to pursue big dreams and goals if you live in a country like the United States or if you were lucky enough to be born into a wealthy family. Sure, the circumstances you were born and raised under can make a difference, but only in the number and types of challenges you face and the opportunities you have. It is entirely possible to pursue your dreams and goals if your circumstances are less than ideal. It may not be as easy, but it sure is possible!

There are a lot of great examples in our recent history of people who overcame difficult times and achieved enormous success. Think of folks like Dolly Parton, who came from a world of extreme poverty.

Oprah Winfrey also came from poverty and was appallingly abused during her childhood. Richard Branson has severe dyslexia, and Steve Jobs was given up for adoption and had a difficult relationship with his adoptive parents. There are numerous stories of successful, happy people who overcame difficult circumstances and achieved their dreams and goals.

For every story of triumph over tough situations, there is a story of someone who had the best of everything growing up but never learned to have dreams and goals and ended up squandering their good fortune, never doing much of anything of value with their life. I want you to be the person who, no matter what's going on in your life, has dreams and goals. Remember, even if you never achieve your exact goal, you can have an awful lot of fun trying if you keep pushing forward and believe in yourself. Speaking of which …

Yes, I hated skiing that first miserable day, but luckily, I stuck with it and ended up loving it so much that I came up with my BHAG of joining the US Olympic Team as a champion ski racer. My stepdad had gotten us involved in the Southern California Junior Ski Racers, and we loved it, but it was a lot of work. The coaches thought I was good but told me that if I wanted to be a champion skier, I'd have to put my all into it and practice year-round. How was I going to do that, since there wasn't snow year-round where I lived? I would have to go someplace like the glaciers in Europe or South America where skiing is available during the summer and at different times of the year.

"I can do that," I thought. "Why not?"

My sister's ex-boyfriend Mickey also loved the idea and the two of us hatched a plan to sail to South America on an old twenty-one-foot sloop my stepdad Ken owned. The problem was that I didn't know how to sail, and neither did Mickey. So, we did a little self-teaching in Newport Bay, and when we felt like we were good enough we sailed to the Coast Guard office to get some information. We told the guys our plan and every single Coast Guardsman in that office immediately burst out laughing. I mean, bent over double, faces red, unable to contain themselves.

Ken's 21-foot sloop

"We saw you sail in here and there's no way you'd make it to South America. You might make it out of the harbor, though!" More laughter. They told us that it would take six months for an experienced sailor to make it to South America in the boat we had. Mickey and I left with our tails between our legs, feeling embarrassed and disheartened. Hey, we were teenagers, what did we know? After recognizing that it was a stupid idea, Mickey and I put our heads together to devise a better plan.

After a little brainstorming, we came up with the idea of using my dad's 1945 World War II Jeep. By now it was 1963, so the Jeep had some age on it, but it was in pretty good shape considering it was almost twenty years old. We started working on the Jeep, but after doing a little more research we found out that it rains a lot in Central America and the northern part of South America.

1945 Jeep

Ross and I prepare the VW bus

Since the Jeep had a cloth top, we knew that wasn't going to work. Back to the drawing board. Notice that we didn't just give up on our plans. We kept at it, trying to figure out a way to get it done. That's what I mean about the importance of believing in yourself and never giving up!

We went to my stepdad for advice and told him that we needed something we could sleep in without getting wet. He said that they had some old Volkswagen buses the school used for student transport that we could buy. We were back in business! We drew up some plans for making the bus travel-friendly, and we got to work. I bought the bus with 80,000 miles on it for $400 from Ken. (More on that later in the book.) We installed cabinets, bunks, and a little stove. We couldn't fit a refrigerator, so we planned to use ice for cooling. After a lot of hard work, we were satisfied that our little traveling house would do us just fine. And then we found out about the travel documents we'd need. When you travel to South America, you need visas and carnets, and those cost a lot of money. Another roadblock!

We eventually got the money together and two weeks before we were to depart, Mickey came to me looking very sheepish. "I can't go," he said. What?! It turned out that Mickey had gotten his girlfriend pregnant, and since he wasn't the type of guy to turn his back on a situation like that, he decided to do the right thing and marry her. I was devastated. How could I possibly go now?

I couldn't make the trip alone, so I started calling all my high school friends, and one after the other they declined. Most felt it was too dangerous, and the ones who wanted to join me didn't have the money. I felt so defeated. I'd bought the Volkswagen bus, converted it, stocked it with supplies for the trip, and gotten all my shots and visas. I couldn't see how I could go without a traveling companion.

I went to Ken in tears, and after he listened to my troubles, he calmly said, "How badly do you want to go? You know the process. What are you going to do? Tell me your plan."

Well, I didn't really have a plan, but after talking to Ken, I knew I had to find someone to go with me. No one from my high school could go, so I came up with the idea of posting flyers at all the colleges in the area to advertise for a travel buddy. Surprisingly, I got a lot of replies from girls, but I didn't want the inevitable entanglements that came with spending months in close quarters with a female.

Eventually, two guys from Illinois who were attending Santa Ana College contacted me and they were all in. I met with Jim and Ross and although they were a little older than me—twenty-one and twenty-two—they were completely gung-ho and they had the time and money to do it. It took a while for them to get their visas and shots, but two weeks after my high school graduation on June 30, 1963, I was on the road and heading to South America!

About forty seconds after we pulled out of my driveway, Jim and Ross began searching for a liquor store. Uh oh. What have I gotten myself into? I wasn't a drinker but was certainly familiar with the effects that alcohol has on people's behavior and judgment. A little tickle of concern started playing around in my brain as we began our adventure, but I was determined! After loading up several cases of Schlitz beer my concern grew, but at least we were once again on our way.

We ran into our first of many predicaments when we reached the Mexican border and the guards searching our bus found my .22 rifle and bullets. We had stupidly decided to bring the gun for protection and possibly for hunting if food got scarce. Not a good idea, it turns out. We hadn't tried to hide the gun; it was in plain sight and I guess that's why we didn't get into any trouble.

The guards just told us to get rid of it; we could not bring the gun into Mexico. I wasn't thrilled with the idea of ditching my gun, so Jim, Ross, and I put our heads together and came up with a solution. We turned around and drove back north until we found an out-of-the-way spot in a tiny town and buried the gun and bullets. Pretty clever, don't you think?

And keep in mind, this was 1963 when gun control wasn't even in the dictionary. We were not as dumb as you may be thinking. Believe it or not, when our adventure was over, and we were headed home, we went back to that spot and there were my gun and bullets, just as we'd left them! When you run into obstacles along your way, you have to get creative, and this is a good example of problem-solving on the fly. I was continuing to learn never to take a defeatist attitude because there's usually a solution if you stay confident and use what's between your ears.

I do wish I'd used as much brain power when I was originally gathering the gun and bullets from the bus to bury them. A stray bullet escaped my notice, and later in the trip when we got to Guatemala, the guards found one .22 bullet in the van. Guatemala had recently had a military uprising and tensions were high, so when they found the bullet, they pulled us aside, searched the van again, and spent hours grilling us. Luckily, they realized that a couple of kids from the States tooling around in an old VW bus with just one bullet wasn't a cause for concern and they let us go.

We continued south without incident through El Salvador and Honduras until we arrived at the border of Nicaragua. We were traveling on the Pan-American highway, which isn't much of a highway in a lot of places. There were stretches of bumpy, two-lane roads and because we weren't paying attention, we didn't see a border crossing. We drove right through it and the next thing we knew we heard a barrage of machine gun fire.

Oh my God! I'm pretty sure the guards weren't trying to hit us; it seemed they were firing up into the air to scare us. We'd heard about bandits roaming around, and we were in a panic not knowing if we should stop or not. Lucky for us, we decided we'd better stop. We told the guards that we hadn't seen the crossing and fortunately they let us pass through without further gunfire. Whew, dumb gringos!

As we traveled south, we were often in awe of the beauty of the Central American landscape, but when we got close to the rain forests near San José, the capital of Costa Rica, we noticed that everything was covered with ash and the skies were full of smoke. It turned out that Mount Irazú, an active volcano, had been erupting for several months, covering everything with thick, gray ash. Most sane people would hightail it in the opposite direction, so what did we decide to do? Drive up to the volcano, of course! We were warned about the danger of sulfur gas and smoke (never mind the real chance for an eruption), but no one tried to stop us.

We got to the top edge, and I suggested walking down the crater to see the inside of the volcano. Jim wasn't keen on that, so Ross and I went on and Jim manned the video camera. At the very edge, I wanted to look way down, so Ross held onto my belt as I leaned forward to get a better view. When it was Ross's turn to look, I held his belt and just as he leaned forward, an earthquake hit. It knocked us to the ground and scared the living daylights out of us. We took off running and got to the bus just as the molten rocks started blasting into the air. Our van suffered two strikes, and we left Mount Irazú in a big hurry in a bus with two holes in the top.

Me at Mount Irazú

Under the category of "never a dull moment," we had our next mishap soon after the volcano incident. As you know, Central America is in the tropics, so it's always hot and humid. I thought I was familiar with hot weather, but this was like hot weather on steroids! We had no air-conditioning in the bus, so we often slept with the doors open even though tarantulas and other large and hairy spiders would enter to keep us company. They frightened us to death, but it was just too hot to sleep with the doors closed.

One night we were awakened by a noise that sounded a little too loud for a spider to make and saw a man running from the bus with a bag he'd grabbed from the van as we slept. We had stupidly put all our passports and money into one place for safekeeping, and that's the bag the thief took off with. In a panic, we ran around until we spotted a police officer, who followed the thief and caught up with him.

We were really fortunate to get our bag back, but the incident ended up delaying our trip by several days because we had to wait for the thief to appear in court so we could identify him. Finally, we got our passports and money back. Months later, on our way home, we stopped to ask the police what had ever happened to the guy. Well, he was given a twenty-year prison sentence, and although what he did was wrong, I still felt sick to my stomach thinking of what a harsh penalty he had received.

Once we were back on the road, we had to deal with the fact that south of Panama was an area filled with jungles, swamps, and even headhunters (or so we heard) and it was impassable, as it still is today. Luckily, I knew while planning this adventure we would have to catch a freighter from Panama to Colombia. We found an Italian tramp steamer on its last sailing that would be leaving in a couple of days but were faced with the higher-than-expected cost of our tickets and the price of shipping the van with us.

Loading the bus on a ship

We also learned about a large band of criminals who had recently ambushed a Colombian military patrol and were now terrorizing and torturing civilians on tourist buses, causing all kinds of problems in Colombia. We decided to change our plans and arranged to sail to Guayaquil, Ecuador, and bypass Colombia. After we figured out the finances and were patting ourselves on the back for being so clever and lucky to be able to ship out without much delay, we found out that they had to load the van the day before we were to leave and that meant we would have no place to sleep that night. Now what?! We were on a very tight budget and could not afford a hotel or even a hostel.

We wandered around trying to figure out what to do and as luck would have it, being in the American Canal Zone, we ran into an American police officer who offered to put us up for the night. We were elated and agreed to meet him at the Canal Zone Jail when he got off his shift at ten o'clock that night. Visions of soft beds with clean linens, hot showers, and a hearty breakfast danced in our heads. But that didn't happen. No, our new friend, the officer, didn't invite us to accompany him to his cozy home; instead, he showed us to some empty jail cells with hard metal bunks and invited us to make ourselves comfortable.

He advised us to be up and out of the jail before the shift changed at six o'clock the next morning, or we might be mistaken for prisoners and be detained indefinitely. Of course, none of us slept well between the miserably uncomfortable cots and the fear of sleeping past six o'clock in the morning and spending the next few years in a Panama prison. After a wretched night, we made our way to our cabin on the ship; it was more cramped and rundown, but the food was great!

Four days later we arrived in Ecuador and continued our journey south through Peru without any real trouble until we reached Lima. There we found ourselves in the middle of a Communist rally and an enormous gun-toting crowd was shooting their guns in the air chanting, "*¡Matar a los Yanquis en Perú!*"

We finally found someone who translated this and found out it meant "Kill the Yankees in Peru!"

Shortly afterward someone asked us where we were from, and all three of us said in unison, "We're Canadian!" Sometimes we were pretty smart gringos!

When I look back now, I realize how dangerous our trip was, especially during the early 1960s when there was a lot of distrust and upheaval. The friends who'd declined my invitation to join me felt it was too dangerous, but to me, it was just an adventure. I confess that I didn't mention a lot of the things that happened when I wrote letters to my family back home. I didn't want them to worry.

Our misadventures continued when that very night we were robbed once again. We had taken the precaution of separating our money from our passports, so this time we only lost most of our money, but it was another devastating blow. My money was in traveler's checks, but Jim and Ross were carrying cash. We ended up with only one hundred dollars left between the three of us and were looking at a two-week delay before I could get reimbursed from the traveler's checks.

I was starting to get very worried. We still had to drive over 2,000 miles on very bad roads to reach Santiago, Chile, and I was concerned that by the time we got there, the snow would have melted. Skiing in Chile was the primary purpose of our long journey, and there was no way I was going to allow us to miss that. We'd had so many delays, and I didn't want to wait any longer, so we talked it out and decided that since gas was so cheap and we had some food, we would have our money sent to the US Embassy in Santiago, Chile, figuring we could make it there. We decided to take the most direct route through the Atacama Desert, and it nearly cost us our lives.

As we made our way south over roads that were so treacherous they could barely be called roads, we heard a loud pop and the bus just stopped. We could tell it was something major and knew it wasn't a good thing to happen in the middle of the Atacama Desert, the driest place on Earth where it hadn't rained in over five hundred years.

We had broken down on a road where there were no other cars, just the occasional truck that came by two or three times a day at this time of year. We tried to wave down the first one, but he just blasted right past us, probably afraid we would rob him if he stopped. We were stranded there all day and night, and on the second day, we knew that we had to do something or we would die out there. It was hot and supplies were getting low, so we put our heads together (again!) and tried to come up with a plan.

I had packed a heavy tow rope in the van, so we got the idea to stand in the middle of the dirt road, wave someone down, and ask them if they could tow us to the nearest town. The first guy who stopped refused, so I came up with the idea to get the next person to stop a little past us and while I talked to him, Jim and Ross would tie the rope onto his truck, leaving him little choice but to tow us. It worked! The fellow knew we wouldn't take no for an answer and begrudgingly agreed to tow us to the next town a few hours away.

It was a scary ride to Quillagua, one of the only towns in that part of the Atacama, and by the time we got there all three of us were feeling really sick. We were running very low on food and were ravenously hungry. Jim and Ross were fed up with me because it was "my dumb bus that had broken down" and I was feeling very low. They took off somewhere, and I just sat in the bus feeling the worst I'd ever felt.

I was so hungry and depressed, but I decided to stop wallowing in my misery and walk around just to change my attitude. I saw a tiny restaurant and when I looked in the window, I noticed that a family had just gotten up to leave, but there was still food on the table. I don't know what I was thinking but I walked right in like I owned the place, grabbed some of the leftovers with two hands, and ran back to the bus. It was fish—I hate fish—but I was so hungry and needed to eat something, so I just devoured it like a wild animal.

That little act did not help me feel any better. I had reached a new low and felt so desperately alone. I tried my best to remember the lessons Ken had taught me about finding solutions and never giving up, but I just couldn't. I had hit rock bottom, so I sat down and wrote a letter to my mom and dad. I poured out my heart to them, telling them how bad things were. It was a letter I have always regretted writing because it ended up causing my parents untold worry and fear for my safety.

It was then that I decided to pray. I mean really pray. I hadn't prayed in years, but I needed it now. I spilled it all out in my prayer, how my buddies were ready to kill me, that I didn't know how we were going to get out of there, that we'd run out of money, that we had no way to fix the bus, and that the snow was melting! When Jim got back to the bus, he and I talked for a short time making silly wishes. I told him about my prayer and how I wished for a place to stay that had showers and free meals. Jim said he would settle for just a bed and a hot shower. Ross was still too upset to talk with me. We all eventually fell asleep from sheer exhaustion.

When I woke up, Ross was fumbling around with the stove trying to get it to start. All morning, we were freezing in our sleeping bags because although this was the Atacama Desert, it was still winter down there and the nights got very cold. He finally got it going and fixed coffee and cocoa to warm us up. Once it was warm, we all got up to try and stop a truck to tow us to Antofagasta. This was easier said than done and it turned into a very long day. Finally, around three o'clock that afternoon the second truck we had seen all day pulled up. After pleading, we got him to tow us to Tocopilla, a port town north of Antofagasta.

It was a treacherous journey and more than a little scary. At one point, our brakes were starting to fail, and then I ran over the rope and broke it, requiring us to coast the rest of the way downhill. By the time we reached Tocopilla, our brakes were gone, and I was really worried, but we miraculously made it. Now here comes the amazing thing. From that point on, after praying harder than I ever thought possible, things only got better!

We found and thanked the truck driver and took a walk around the little town. We ran into an American who worked for the Chillax Corporation, a part of Anaconda Copper. I explained our dilemma to him, and he introduced us to Mr. Pope, the Chilean American chief engineer at Chillax. Mr. Pope immediately took us under his wing and got one of their trucks, loaded us on it, and took us to the apartment complex they kept for visiting US dignitaries. We were given an apartment that to us looked like a five-star hotel where we could shower and sleep in a real bed. They even fed us! It was a lifesaver, and we couldn't believe our good fortune.

Getting towed out of the desert

The next day they took our bus into their shop, took it apart, and discovered it had a snapped crankshaft. They didn't have the facilities or parts to fix a Volkswagen, so Mr. Pope had them load the bus back onto their truck and take us down to a Volkswagen shop in Antofagasta, Chile. He and Mrs. Pope also gave us the names of a couple of their friends George and Martin in Antofagasta who also took us under their wings. Because of Chile's Independence Day, it would take over two weeks for them to get the parts they needed to repair the bus, so we were stranded again. But this time, we had a place to stay, people fixing our bus, and two exceptional new friends who fed us and took care of us in extraordinary ways.

On the third or fourth day in Antofagasta, a bunch of military guys approached us, armed with their AK-47s.

"We're looking for David Jackson," one said. I told them I was David and they immediately grabbed me by the arms and said, "Come with us."

They wouldn't let Jim or Ross come with me, and I was pretty terrified as they walked me into the colonel's office.

The colonel looked at me and said, "Are you David Jackson?"

I told him I was. "Call your mother, she is sick!" he said.

I was flabbergasted and more than a little relieved that I wasn't in trouble. It turned out that my mother wasn't technically ill, she was just sick with worry. After she'd received my letter, she called the US Ambassador to Chile and told him that her son was down there in Chile, was dying, and needed to be rescued. She convinced them to conduct a search and rescue around Tocopilla, which is where I'd mailed the letter. Somehow or another they found me and thankfully put an end to my mother's worries.

Our good fortune continued as we awaited the repairs on the bus. When the bus was finally fixed, the owner of the VW repair facility kindly reduced the charges for labor to only twenty-nine dollars for two weeks of work despite them virtually replacing most of the engine. We were astounded by their generosity and thanked them over and over again.

We'd been delayed three weeks because of the breakdown, so we decided to hightail it down to Santiago to finally go skiing before the snow melted. When we arrived, we were pretty bedraggled, but even though the money from the traveler's checks was waiting for us, we still had a long way to travel and didn't want to spend it on a hotel room. We wanted to go out on the town, so we decided to use a little trick for cleaning ourselves up that I'd seen done in a movie.

Here's how it worked: We went to the Hilton Hotel and walked into the lobby, doing our best to pretend we belonged there. We went upstairs and found a room that was unlocked. We went in, used the shower, and changed into our best clean clothes. We donned our Panama hats and walked out of the hotel looking very Western. It worked! No one stopped us and we happily headed out for our night on the town.

I wanted to celebrate fulfilling my BHAG to drive to Santiago, Chile, for adventure and to ski and prepare for the Olympics. I decided to treat Ross and Jim to filet mignon at the Il Bosco steak house in Santiago. To my delight, it only cost me five dollars for the whole delicious meal. Afterward, we went to see *How the West Was Won* and when the film ended and we stood up to leave, everyone in the theater started applauding us because we were Americans and we looked like the characters in the movie. At that time, John F. Kennedy was president, and a lot of people loved him, so they loved us too. It was a great experience and to this day, *How the West Was Won* is still my favorite movie of all time.

After the movie, we ran into an English-speaking guy who took us to a volunteer fire department in Santiago. They offered to let us use the bunks at the fire station so we didn't have to sleep in the bus and even took us on a ride through the town on a hook-and-ladder fire truck. It was awesome! Things like that continued to happen and to this day the Chilean people are my favorites. They are the friendliest, most accommodating people I've ever met anywhere in the world.

We continued on our way, but not without incident. The bus started acting up again. When the mechanics had been working on the VW bus in Antofagasta, they discovered that it hadn't had 80,000 miles on it when we'd left California, it had more than twice that. So, it didn't surprise me when we found a few more problems with a vehicle that had more than 180,000 miles on it. The transmission was leaking and there were other issues, but God didn't quit pouring out blessings on us.

That prayer in the Atacama Desert would not be my last prayer. Everywhere we turned and everyone we met must have been sent from God. We found a repair shop where they fixed our transmission, repaired the gas pump, changed the oil and transmission fluid, and lubed it all for a dollar! God's blessings didn't stop there; they continued throughout the rest of our trip.

The next day we drove up to the Farellones ski area outside of Santiago, and were finally able to hit the slopes! I taught Ross and Jim how to ski and although Ross picked it up right away, Jim just couldn't get the hang of it. To his credit, he kept trying, but never quite figured it out. We skied and skied for five days, and I was in heaven until I developed snow blindness, which is like a sunburn on your eyes. I hadn't been wearing sunglasses, so it was my own stupidity that caused it to happen. I ended up having to stay indoors for three days because my eyes were extremely sensitive to light and so sensitive that even a flickering candle would cause a lot of pain. Still, it was so thrilling to be able to finally ski in Chile, South America!

Me, Ross, and Jim

Our next stop was Portillo, a ski resort legendary for its enchanted Lake of the Inca. Depending on the conditions, the color of the water in this magical lake changes from the deepest blue to a shimmering emerald green. It was gorgeous! While on the way there, we were introduced to some friendly Chilean Mormons who not only got us a free ride on the train to Portillo but let us park our bus in a safe place for a few days.

While in Portillo, the Chilean military let us bunk down in their barracks, which was fortunate because we couldn't afford a hotel. I've said it before and I'll say it again, the friendliest, most accommodating people I've ever met are the Chileans. Even their military is welcoming! Unfortunately, Mother Nature wasn't as agreeable as the Chileans and the weather warmed up, causing the snow to turn into mush. Time to leave Portillo and head to Argentina!

Since we weren't permitted to drive our bus into Argentina—the government didn't want anyone entering the country with vehicles they might intend to sell—we decided to hitchhike across the Andes and on to Argentina, Uruguay, and Brazil. We didn't know what to do with our bus and didn't have any bags to pack our clothes in, but a solution quickly presented itself in the form of a couple of military guys we ran into. We told them our story, and they not only offered to give us their military backpacks, they even pulled a tank out of its garage and parked our VW bus there! They told us that the only way to get to Argentina was by rail, and advised us to hop on a freight train, which we attempted.

After barely making it onto the train as it departed, a conductor caught us and kicked us off. Embarrassed and sore, we bought tickets for the next train. The train cars were a real mess, but all that mattered was that we were on our way to Argentina. At the next stop, we were able to hitchhike on a just-emptied cattle truck and spent the next several hours holding our noses, sitting on a small piece of hay to avoid the residue from the departed cattle. It smelled pretty gross, and we found ourselves wondering if this was going to be worth it. We hitchhiked and were given rides in every kind of vehicle you can imagine. We even rode on a horse cart that was carrying a bunch of bottles. It was a pretty awesome adventure!

Unfortunately, we didn't find the Argentine people nearly as friendly or helpful as our Chilean friends. However, it seemed my prayer continued to open other doors. When we arrived in Buenos Aires, Ross was prompted to try to reach his ex-girlfriend Stevie from Illinois who he thought now lived in Buenos Aires. As it happened, she was in town and invited us to her parents' home. When we arrived, I guess we looked pretty bad because she about dropped dead when she saw us. Her mother had the same reaction, but welcomed us anyway and invited us to shower.

After we were all cleaned up, we had a wonderful dinner with the family followed by one of the best night's sleeps we'd had in a long time. The next day we were invited to the annual American picnic where we feasted on the most delicious Argentine food. While we were eating, the US Ambassador asked us over to meet him. We talked to Mr. McClinock and also met the president of Esso Oil of South America and the Assistant US Ambassador.

We left Buenos Aires rested, very satisfied, and feeling pretty important since the local newspaper published an article and pictures of us. After another relaxing day spent feasting on barbecued steaks and a second night of dancing with Stevie's beautiful American friends, we left to inch our way up to Rio de Janeiro, a place I've always wanted to visit.

When we got to Rio, I called some acquaintances of my mom who lived there and were invited to their apartment. The woman was a Danish beauty with a jealous Czech husband who left work to come right home when his wife told him we were visiting. She invited us to shower and stay, but her husband said we would probably be happier meeting some of their American friends at an American school nearby.

We stayed at the school for the next four days, partying with the Americans and more good-looking Brazilian girls than we had seen in a long time. They took us to the Copacabana nightclub each night and we ran into a really nice Brazilian guy who showed us all the beautiful Rio sites. He convinced me to drink rum and Coke and for the first and only time in my life, I got more than a little tipsy. We were really lucky that we didn't lose our money or get robbed, but due to the judgment-reducing effects of alcohol, we did end up with two monkeys, a male and a female.

Clearly, it was a stupid thing to do. How would we ever get monkeys back to the United States? As it turned out, we were amazingly successful in getting both of them across three borders but sadly, we didn't have to sneak them around anymore after we got caught in a late fall blizzard. We were in the Andes Mountains on the way back to Chile when the storm hit. Without any place to stay, we ended up sleeping in an abandoned building.

It was bitterly cold and we tried our best to keep each other warm, but although we survived the night, the monkeys didn't make it. We named them Andy and Andrea before burying them in the snow and waited for the next train to continue to Chile where we picked up our bus and thanked our military and Mormon friends who helped us so much. I've always felt bad about the fate of Andy and Andrea, however.

Because of the blizzard, we managed to get a few extra days of skiing in, and then it was time to head home for Christmas. We drove straight through as we made our way up the coast of South America and back to Peru, where we decided to take a long detour to see Lake Titicaca, Bolivia, and Machu Picchu. It was quite a detour, but we felt it would be worth it and that's why we chose to take the shortest route, which went over the highest navigable pass in the world at an altitude of 18,000 feet.

Machu Picchu

We were told that it wasn't a wise idea to try to take that route because of the lack of oxygen for both our engine and our lungs, but we went ahead and did it anyway. Well, whoever advised us against it was right. The bus could barely move, we could hardly breathe, and we ended up with a flat tire. Working as a team to change the flat, I jumped on top of the bus to retrieve the spare tire, Ross jacked the bus up, and Jim loosened the lug nuts. Wow! All of us almost passed out from that simple exertion. We just couldn't breathe. I felt so helpless and didn't know what to do.

Suddenly, out of nowhere, an old man and his wife walked toward us and gestured, asking if we needed help. I nodded yes, and the old fellow had that tire changed in minutes. He was an Inca descendant who lived high up in the mountains, so his lungs were acclimated, unlike ours. I was so grateful for his help, and I still have a photo of him, holding an old flintlock gun and looking just like the savior he was.

After Machu Picchu, we made it back to Guayaquil, Ecuador, just in time to catch the old tramp steamer *Amerigo Vespucci* on its final run home. While on the ship we heard a call from the radio room saying that President Kennedy had been assassinated. We couldn't believe it. When we arrived in Panama a few days later, everything was draped in black and we learned that Lee Oswald, Kennedy's assassin, had been killed. It sounded like the country was falling apart, and we were anxious to get home.

We didn't make as many stops on the way back to California but managed one last stay in Acapulco for some much-needed rest. While there, we were lucky to see thirty-five Acapulco cliff divers during a special holiday dive and it was fantastic! We splurged on a hotel room that cost three dollars a night and included three mediocre meals. We didn't stay there long; I was anxious to get going. I wanted to be home for Christmas and most of all, I wanted to surprise my parents.

It was the nineteenth of December when I arrived back home to Santa Ana, and I couldn't wait to execute my clever idea of sneaking into the house and letting my parents find me sleeping in my bed the next morning. I crept up the stairs and got about halfway when I saw my stepdad standing at the top with his gun cocked. I thought, "Holy crap, all this stuff that could have happened in South America, and I am going to get shot in my own house!" I found out later that my mom's former boyfriend had been threatening my parents to the point that my dad started keeping a gun near his bed for security. After that close call, I vowed never to have a gun in my house.

My incredible South American adventure had a life-changing impact on my future. When I left California to begin that journey, I wasn't in the habit of praying much, but that prayer in the Atacama Desert turned almost everything around. I could feel God's influence and came to believe in God even more during that trip. We had a guardian angel following us through our travels.

When I look back, I realize there were so many times I could have given up: When we were nearly killed by a volcano, robbed several times, lost three weeks of skiing time due to breakdowns, faced the Communist threats in Peru, almost froze to death with our monkeys in the Andes, and more. There was only one time that I thought seriously about giving up on that dream when everything and everyone was against me in the Atacama Desert. It was the worst day of this trip and of my life up until then.

That prayer saved me and changed me forever and the confidence instilled in me by my stepdad was increased due to those often very challenging experiences. I strengthened my resolve to not give up on my dreams, ever! I'd reached my BHAG of skiing in the summer, driving all the way to Santiago, Chile, hitchhiking to Rio, and so much more. This was the beginning of a new BHAG: to ski and travel the world.

LOOKS CAN BE DECEIVING, SO USE YOUR NOSE

Our first experience in South America happened just a few minutes after getting off the ship in Guayaquil, Ecuador. We got stuck so badly in what we thought was a mudhole that we needed a lot of help to get us out. We were able to get ten men to slosh in the mud for half an hour to try to get us out. We then realized that it was a sewage hole, and even though we had just showered on the ship before getting off, we badly needed to shower again. We all really stunk!

BHAG GENERATOR

In this chapter, I shared the seeds of my own spiritual journey that came about because of my BHAG dream and adventure. When I prayed for help in the desert and saw my prayers answered, it changed the course of my life. Think about your own spirituality and list some instances in your life when you felt you received a helping hand.

____

____

____

____

____

4

BIG DECISIONS

After returning from The Great South American Adventure, it was time to get back to the real world, and I had to decide what I was going to do next. I knew I needed to go to college, and after discussing it with my parents, I chose to go to Fullerton, a community college not far from my home in Santa Ana.

As you know, I struggled in school for many years, but I always did pretty well in math, so I started taking calculus and physics courses. While attending Fullerton, I was also working at the local Carl's Jr. where I began to meet a lot of cute college girls. Back in those days, there weren't many girls in the math classes, and I welcomed the female attention I found at Carl's Jr. I had never dated much, but my trip to South America and getting my pilot's license had upped my self-confidence, so I dove right in. I would pick up dates in the VW van I'd driven to South America and impress the girls by showing them the map of all the countries I'd visited.

Jim, Ross, and me back home

When I think back to those days, I realize that trying new things, going on adventures, and pushing myself past what I thought I was capable of boosted my self-confidence. If you just try different things, you may surprise yourself when you find out how much is possible! Start keeping your eyes and ears open for opportunities and grab them. You'll be amazed at how many opportunities become available to you if you just ask. It never hurts to ask, and the worst thing that can happen is that someone will say no.

As I went along working, going to school, and dating, I never lost my desire to ski and still dreamed of becoming an Olympian. But skiing was expensive, and I wasn't making very much money; I had to figure something out. During a family ski trip to Mammoth, I noticed some young guys punching lift tickets and I got to talking to them. I found out that the owner of the ski resort, Dave McCoy, allowed them to ski for free in the afternoons if they worked on the ticket line in the mornings. The wheels in my head immediately began spinning and a plan started to form in my mind.

The skiing up at Mammoth Mountain was so much better than the skiing in Southern California, and they always had more snow. I figured that if I was going to pursue my dream of becoming an Olympic skier, I'd have to ski at least every weekend, and that wasn't possible where I lived since the first snow-making machine wasn't put into service at Big Bear until several years later.

After finding a way to ski for free, I had to figure out where I could stay in Mammoth. I sure couldn't afford a hotel room! The VW bus seemed to be a perfect solution, but it already had over two hundred thousand miles on it, and its larger interior would be more difficult to keep warm for sleeping. I needed to find a way to do this as cheaply as possible and had to factor in the cost of gas for the twelve-hour round trip to and from Mammoth.

I ended up buying a used station wagon and installing a mattress and a little heater in the back. I put the word out to my ski friends and always found someone willing to pay for the gas in exchange for the luxury accommodations (i.e., the mattress in the rear of my station wagon). My friends or my brother Bob and I would raid our parents' refrigerators for food and be on our way. All in all, it worked out, although there were a couple of frigid nights where I thought we might freeze to death. But we didn't, and the plan allowed me to ski for free all winter.

It's important for me to share the Mammoth story so you can see that by being a little creative and doing some brainstorming, solutions are often a lot easier than you might think. Don't abandon your dreams and goals without spending some time figuring out a way to make them possible. You have to adjust, think outside the box, and search for opportunities to make your dreams come true. A lot more is possible than you might think! It shocked me how working hard, not giving up, and asking even if you're convinced the answer would be no led to my being able to fulfill so many dreams.

As I look back at those times, I believe God had a big part in my striving for goals and taking advantage of opportunities that came my way. I believe all of us can find a lot more opportunities in life than most people think. They are there! You have to keep striving to find them and be willing to take a leap of faith.

My next big opportunity presented itself in November 1964. I was still attending Fullerton College when my sister Susan invited me to homecoming at Brigham Young University. She loved BYU; she'd made a lot of friends; she adored her teachers and—here comes the clincher—the skiing in Utah was fantastic.

While I was there, Susan set me up on dates and then introduced me to the captain of the BYU ski team, Gary Andrus. I was having a terrific time and was struck by the friendliness of not only the students but of everyone I met there. It didn't hurt that the co-eds were some of the most beautiful women I'd ever seen. Susan had told Gary about my interest in skiing and Gary said that if I was as good as she said I was, I would easily make the ski team if I transferred there. I was a little hesitant because BYU was sponsored by the Church of Jesus Christ of Latter-day Saints, and I didn't want anything to do with religion at the time. But then I found out that the ski team skied every day except Sunday, and that was what sold me on transferring to BYU.

I was accepted for the next semester, which was in January of 1965. Gary helped me arrange my schedule; I took early morning classes so we could be at Timp Haven (now Sundance) ski resort every weekday to practice with our coaches. The whole team, except for a couple of the active church members, skied on the weekends at Park City where we were able to get cheap college season passes.

We tore up the slopes so enthusiastically that we were occasionally warned to slow down or we'd lose our passes. It was a dream come true! I worked as hard as I ever have in my life to get into the best physical shape for the upcoming races. Since I had only started skiing when I was a teenager, I was really behind the other racers and ended up finishing at the very bottom of the competitions. It was so embarrassing, but it was also a good wake-up call, telling me that I'd have to work even harder if I had any chance of fulfilling my dream of making the Olympic ski team. I improved but never finished near the top.

1965 BYU ski team (I am second from right)

It was at a large competition in Jackson Hole, Wyoming, that I had a chance to ski with real Olympians. The event included most of the 1960 and 1964 Olympic teams, and I was thrilled beyond words to be able to ski against racers like Jimmie Heuga, the 1964 Olympic bronze medalist, and Billy Kidd, the silver medalist. I knew I'd never win the race but thought that if I placed in the top third, I could prove to myself, my teammates, and the coaches that I still had a chance to make the Olympic team.

During the downhill race, the most dangerous of all the Olympic races, my nerves started to get the better of me. I tried to follow my coach's advice to visualize the course, but all I could think of was crashing and breaking every bone in my body. As I stood at the starting gate, I heard a radio squawk and the words, "Oh no! He crashed! Oh, it's bad, I hope he's OK." This was the worst possible thing for me to hear as I stood there watching my life flash before my eyes.

To add to my anxiety, the accident delayed my start by a few minutes, giving me more time to worry about whether I'd make it to the bottom of the hill in one piece. I tried to calm myself and imagined Ken's soothing voice asking me, "How badly do you want this?" Unfortunately, the voice in my head was bellowing, "DO YOU WANT TO DIE?"

At that moment the countdown began, and as I took off, all I could imagine was my fellow racer lying in the snow, broken and bleeding. I pulled it together, managing not to join the twenty-five others who fell, and made it through the course, finishing in the bottom 20 percent. Although disappointed in placing so low, I was filled with relief that I had made it down the hill without killing myself or breaking multiple bones.

While at Jackson Hole, I had a chance to talk with the other racers about my goal of making the Olympic team. They pointed out that I'd started way too late to achieve that goal; most of them had started skiing when they were toddlers. They also told me that to be an Olympic skier, you had to devote your entire life to skiing and to all aspects of preparation for the races. That meant no girlfriends, no part-time jobs, no college, just working out and skiing. It was also a very expensive proposition since I wouldn't be able to generate any income while in training. I was starting to realize that my dream of making the Olympics might have started too late in life.

The realization that I'd have to give up so much, including my dreams of making enough money to buy my own jet since I couldn't become a fighter pilot, made me rethink this particular BHAG. It seemed that my goal of becoming an Olympic skier would be nearly impossible to achieve. However, I was always keeping my eyes and ears open for more opportunities and before I knew it, another one popped up.

Shortly after returning from Jackson Hole, my parents called to tell me that they'd bought out their partners in the Chateau Après Ski Lodge in Park City, Utah that they had just built and opened that year, and needed a manager for the summer while they tried to find someone full time. Would I be interested? I had to make the big decision to abandon my dreams of skiing in the Olympics, and I knew it was time to change my path. Of course, my mind immediately zeroed in on the word "ski," and so I said yes. I was awed by the idea that my parents would trust me, a twenty-year-old, to manage their ski lodge, but I felt confident that I could handle it. As I look back, I think that God was urging me to create a new BHAG and let go of one that I knew in my heart wasn't going to happen.

In April 1965, right after the school term ended, I began my next adventure of managing a thirty-two-room lodge, a small troop of employees, a full-sized restaurant, and a bar. If I hadn't had the successes I'd had with the South America trip, getting my pilot's license, working with Ken Holt at Fairmont, working at the airport, and racing at Jackson Hole, I doubt I would have had the self-confidence to accept such a demanding position.

But as I mentioned before, everything you do to challenge yourself, every risk you take, and every push you give yourself results in building your confidence. That's why I encourage you to always go ahead and try new things. No one succeeds 100 percent of the time, so why should you expect that of yourself? If you work hard, think creatively, and believe in yourself, you can do a lot more than you'd ever imagined.

Me at Chateau Après front desk

1965 Chateau Après Lodge, with the Corvette and VW bus

So, there I was, at twenty years of age and not even legally old enough to drink, buying kegs of beer and bottles of wine for the lodge. Sometimes when I think back, I am amazed I had the nerve to do some of the things I did! Since it was springtime, there weren't any skiers at the lodge, so my workload wasn't too bad. We kept the lodge open through the summer, and people would come up to play golf and enjoy the beautiful scenery. I only had three employees to manage, and I was responsible for cleaning the rooms and manning the front desk.

We had enough guests staying at the lodge and enough local residents dining at the restaurant to keep it open, and I only had to oversee a maid, a cook and a waitress. It was a great way to get my feet wet in the hospitality industry, and when my parents asked me if I would be willing to stay on as manager for the fall and winter, I said yes. I was able to continue taking classes at BYU part-time, so I didn't have to choose between managing the lodge and finishing college. I did have to officially give up my quest to make the Olympic team.

I really enjoyed my time managing the ski lodge over the next few years. I had made my final decision not to pursue the Olympics, I had switched my major to business, and I could enjoy skiing in Park City on my days off. I found that I enjoyed recreational skiing more than racing, so I was OK with my decision.

During that first year at the lodge, I was able to save enough money to buy a brand-new silver Corvette because my room and board were free and I could deposit most of my salary into a savings account. I was learning a lot of new things working at the lodge. I learned how to advertise and fill the rooms all winter, I learned how to manage a staff, and I took on the responsibility of both hiring and firing people. I joined the Park City Hotel Association, and not long after I was appointed their vice president. I even became a board member of the Park City Chamber of Commerce!

My 1966 Corvette

Let me stop here and remind you that I was just a regular Joe, an average student, and not particularly gifted in anything at all (although I was a pretty darn good skier). So how did I do all these things in my early twenties? Honestly, I just took that leap of faith to trust and believe in myself. I didn't overthink things and didn't waste time questioning myself. I just did it. Most of the time things worked out fine (and sometimes they didn't) and that is why I want to keep reminding you to just go ahead and try different things because you will certainly surprise yourself. I guarantee it.

OK, back to the ski lodge. I was having a great time in Park City, cruising at breakneck speeds in my Corvette to get to classes at BYU, meeting a lot of great people, and dating a lot of cute girls. I was able to ski when I wasn't working, and I felt confident and successful running the lodge. Life was good, but of course, there was a plan hatching in my head for the future.

I had given up my Olympic dream, but I still wanted to ski in more places and my trip to South America had made me hungry to travel the world. I decided my next goal was to save enough money to spend a few years driving around the world and skiing at as many places as I could. I wanted to see and experience as many places as possible. I immediately started hatching a plan for my next big adventure!

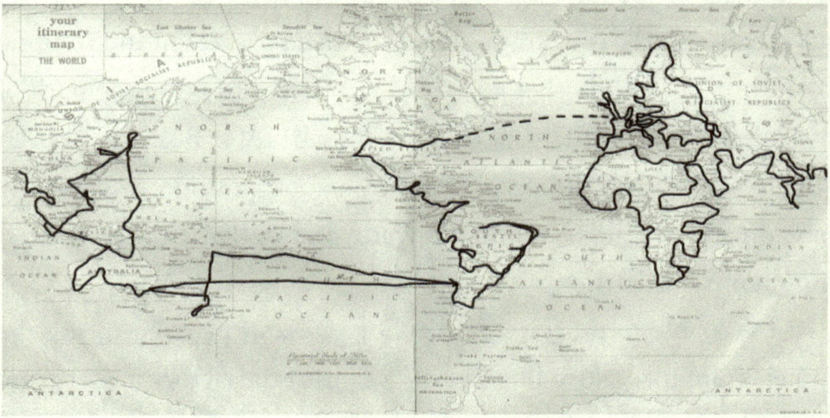

David's 1968 planned world trip

I spent the next three and a half years taking business classes at BYU and applying what I learned to running the ski lodge. I studied the practices of my fellow businessmen and businesswomen in Park City and ended up securing a huge contract with the Big Ten universities to house and feed one hundred geology students for eight weeks every summer at the lodge. This was a big deal since it was always a struggle to generate income at the ski lodge in the off-season, and as it turned out, the program to host the students has lasted over fifty-six years!

All of the experiences I had running the lodge were beneficial to my future business opportunities, and I knew that my decision to change direction—to put aside my Olympic dream and run the lodge—had been the right one. When it comes to BHAGs, I've learned to allow for some flexibility and to never let myself think that I'd failed in achieving this goal or that dream. Again, I encourage you to keep your eyes and ears open for opportunities, don't doubt yourself, and most of all don't be afraid to try new things. You never know what will come of them!

In the fall of 1968, I made the difficult choice to leave my position as manager of the ski lodge. I say it was a difficult choice because it's never easy to walk away from something that's successful and running smoothly. But I had other goals and they were always in the back of my mind. It was time to pursue my next BHAG. Because I'd been able to save so much money, I was in a good position to chase my next dream—to drive around the world and ski some of the greatest mountains on Earth.

I was able to quickly sell the Corvette and planned to use the money from that sale to buy a new VW bus at the factory in Germany and equip it for my adventure. With what I had left from the sale of the Corvette plus my savings I could travel for a year or two before having to work again. I also wanted to find one or two people to accompany me on the trip, so I made a flyer and took it to every university within driving distance. I sent some down to Southern California and had them posted at universities in that area as well.

1968 Drive Around the World flyer

To my shock, most of the responses I got were from girls! Now, as much as I loved the company of girls, I didn't want to travel with a female because I wanted to avoid any complications that might occur, and I felt more comfortable traveling in such close quarters with another guy. Pretty quickly, I found Ralph, a fellow who wanted to join me and had the funds to finance his share of the trip. It was time to get going!

THE WORLD'S BEST CHEF

The ski lodge had a small restaurant, and I usually hired local cooks to prepare the meals. However, I wasn't too happy with their work, so I decided to broaden my scope and advertise in nearby Salt Lake City. I got several applications, but one really stood out. The guy's resume was awesome, so I ended up hiring him, but being a bit inexperienced in the business, I never checked his references. I took him at his word, and he didn't disappoint. He was a fantastic cook and everyone loved him.

He'd been working for us for about a month when someone came to me complaining that he was selling drugs to the other employees. I was stunned; he seemed like such a great guy. I pulled out his resume and called the first name he listed as a reference. To my shock, the fellow who answered the phone told me that my cook was an escaped convict! I immediately called the prison and spoke to the warden, who said that I had to get him back to the prison right away because he was the best cook they'd ever had. "I haven't eaten well since he escaped!" the warden said. When I went to fire him, I found out that he'd disappeared. I don't know whatever happened to him, but we sure missed his cooking after he left. He really was a great chef.

BHAG GENERATOR

The theme of this chapter centers on taking advantage of opportunities. Even if an opportunity might collide with a BHAG, don't just discount it. Think it through, pray about it, and see what would be best for you and your family's overall dreams. Then make your decision. It's not always easy but it will be worth it.

Reflect on an opportunity that you passed on or dreamed about because you were unsure of what the outcome would be. Write down all the opportunities you might have had and then write a few lines about how things might have worked out if you'd taken that opportunity, and what you'd do differently if you had a second chance.

Find some mentors to bounce these ideas or dreams off of to get their feedback. Be aware of and avoid negative mentors. Use this as a reminder not to be afraid to take chances, as long as they're moral, legal, and not too dumb. Be a risk-taker and trust yourself. You will make mistakes, but you will learn from them. I did! You can succeed if you take chances and have faith in yourself.

5

BACK IN THE USSR

Before I begin this chapter, I need to explain my thinking and resolve about not wanting to travel with girls. This was the 1960s, and the Sexual Revolution was in high gear throughout the United States and Europe. I had gone to BYU and learned much more about the Church of Jesus Christ of Latter-day Saints (Mormon or Latter-day Saint [LDS] church). I hadn't requested in prayer or received any confirmation that this church was the correct one for me; I was not ready to start attending any church. But I had received a confirmation that some of their doctrine was right and best for me.

Even in high school I had decided to abstain from tobacco, drugs, and alcohol, and made a strong commitment to myself and to the God I knew at the time that I would never partake of them, mostly for health and economic reasons. I kept that commitment religiously and only faltered that one time in Brazil and later repented for that mistake.

I guess I was already becoming a conservative politically, as I was opposed to the Haight-Ashbury culture of free love, and the antiwar rhetoric that the 1960s had ushered in. I believed what the LDS Church taught—that having sexual relations before marriage was wrong—and I had already been affected by my best friend Mickey's mistake that cost him the trip of a lifetime and almost cost me my BHAG dream. (You might recall that Mickey got his girlfriend pregnant and couldn't join me on the South America trip.)

I was committed to not making the same mistakes I had seen others make. So, my disclaimer is that once I realized that traveling with females and males together worked without the entanglements I was so afraid of, I relaxed my opposition to that restriction. It also made great sense economically. I will explain more about my decision to travel with just one female later in this chapter.

Ralph and I quickly started putting together our plan to leave Southern California for Europe on September 18, 1968. Rather than spending the money to fly to New York and catch a flight to Europe, we found a man who paid us to drive his Italian sports car—a Lancia—to Princeton, New Jersey, and drop it off with his son. We had a great road trip across the country and we saved money. It also allowed me to stop in Ohio and see my dad, Harlan Jackson. Win, win!

We flew from New York to Iceland and from there on to Luxembourg. Ralph wanted to get to Germany in time for Oktoberfest, and even though I didn't drink, it sounded like fun, so I was fine with that. I liked the idea of going to Germany because there were a lot of American military bases there where we could meet other Americans, and as a bonus, we could buy food and supplies at a great discount and get cheap gas coupons.

Oktoberfest was certainly more fun for Ralph than it was for me since he spent most of the time drinking beer. It was really cold, and since we didn't have a van yet, we ended up sleeping in tents that other young foreign travelers had set up near Oktoberfest. I knew it was time to get some transportation, so we went to a factory and ordered a Volkswagen bus. It was going to take a few months to get the bus because of the special equipment I'd ordered that would allow us to live in it as we traveled, so I knew that we needed to find something to drive, sleep, and travel in while we waited. I found a used VW bus for $200, and that solved the problem of accommodations and travel until the new bus was ready.

My $200 VW bus

It took us ten days in Munich to accomplish our search for a few companions to travel to Spain with. I found out that traveling with girls was the norm in Europe, so I revised my thinking and it turned out great! We spent a month with three different girls and a couple of guys from Australia traveling throughout Switzerland, Spain, Monte Carlo, and France, seeing the beautiful sights, and even scuba diving in the Mediterranean Sea.

In Switzerland, we stopped at a beautiful ski town to visit with friends of my parents. While there, we saw a glider flying over the

French Alps, so we stopped in Grenoble, France, and asked around only to find out that I could fly a glider over the Alps for only thirty francs (six US dollars). I hadn't flown in so long and couldn't resist such a temptation, so I paid the money and soared over the Alps for fifteen minutes in a glider. It was fantastic and I loved it!

My glider flight over the French Alps

The snows arrived early that year, and we were able to ski in November. My parents and sister Rebecca came over to ski with me right after Christmas. When I got back to Germany, I met an American girl named Shelagh at a military base in Garmisch. She also loved skiing and was quite good at it, so we spent the next two months, including Christmas, skiing all over the French, Italian, German, and Swiss Alps.

I jokingly brought up the idea of driving through the Soviet Union, skiing in the Soviet Caucasus Mountains, and visiting that exciting and challenging country. To my shock, she agreed. I was happy to have a female traveling companion who was as excited about skiing as I was, had the money to travel, and wasn't afraid to drive through the USSR.

I want to stop here for a moment and explain this decision based on my earlier disclaimer.

Although traveling with girls and guys together had proved very successful without any romantic entanglements, I realized traveling with just one girl could be more challenging. However, I had made a very strong commitment to myself and God and could not find anyone at the time who fit my requirement to travel for up to six months to the USSR.

Shelagh and I had already gotten along very well, and she was also very committed to not getting involved romantically. We did not break that ban and commitment during the times we were together. It was not easy, but I am proud of both of us. Shelagh turned out to be the best travel companion I had ever had until my future wife Stacey came into my life. Stacey has far exceeded Shelagh or anyone else as a travel companion—and much more!

After spending the next two months preparing the new VW bus for this exciting trip and skiing as much as possible, we were ready to go. On February 26, 1969, we left our base in Garmisch and traveled throughout southern Europe, skiing everywhere we could, visiting most of the exciting and exotic places in Southern and Eastern Europe, and eventually making it to the eastern border of Turkey and the USSR. On April 9, we reached the summit of the snow-covered mountains just south of the Black Sea where we met eight rough-looking Turkish road workers who could not speak any English.

Rebecca, Mom, and me skiing the Matterhorn

Despite their scary appearance, they turned out to be friendly and welcoming, sharing their soup, bread, and a big bowl of Turkish stew with us. We attempted to communicate with them in every way we could and soon were able to develop a friendship. We saw them again the next morning and they insisted we have breakfast with them before we began our hike up the mountain to ski. After breakfast, we gathered our gear and began the one-hour hike to the top of the mountain.

Hiking a third of a mile up a mountain wearing ski clothes and carrying ski equipment was no walk in the park, but it was worth it because we got to ski down a beautiful slope covered with deep snow.

The men from the highway department had walked over and cheered us on as we skied past them back to the road. We continued to ski down the mountain as Shelagh and I traded back and forth skiing near the road while the other drove until we got to the bottom of Mount Kop Dağı. It was so much fun! We were pretty sure that no one had ever skied this before and I only wish we would have done it more often. It was a wonderful and exciting time, but things were about to change.

When we got to Kars, a city in northeast Turkey, we found out that the only way to cross into the Soviet Union was by train. We had received permission and a visa from the Soviet Embassy in Switzerland to drive into the Soviet Union from the border town of Kars. We planned to ski in the Caucasus Mountains of Southern Russia and drive through the heart of the USSR, camping in my VW bus along the way to Moscow, then exiting the Soviet Union at the border between Leningrad and Finland in the north.

Preparing to ski in Turkey

We found the old run-down train station in this godforsaken town near the Soviet border where we would catch a Turkish train that left only once a week for the USSR. It would take my VW bus and the two of us from Kars, Turkey to Tbilisi, Georgia in the USSR. We found the train station around ten o'clock in the morning and were surprised when the station manager told us that we could not get the train tickets until the next morning at eight o'clock and that we had to pay in Turkish lira. Since the train was scheduled to leave only an hour after we'd gotten our tickets, I was a little worried about the timing but had no choice except to leave and go back the next morning.

As we were leaving the ticket station, we ran into a local teacher named Hassan who spoke some English. We told him we had to exchange our American dollars for Turkish lira to buy the train tickets and asked if he could help us. He was nice enough to accompany me to the bank, where I did the exchange. Hassan then invited us to lunch with him at his home. He lived in a run-down one-room shack with his charming wife and two small children, cooking and heating the house with an old coal stove. In the corner of the room was a typical Turkish toilet consisting of a small hole in the floor. It was all so depressing, but they were considered Turkish middle income, and incredibly, they were much better off than some others! Hassan said, "I'm not poor and I'm not rich but just in between."

Friendly Turkish road crew

After enjoying a huge Turkish lunch prepared by Hassan's wife, who didn't join us to eat, by the way, we went back to the ticket station where I was now told I would have to pay for the tickets in American dollars! This day just kept getting worse and worse. We went back to the bank where the head teller, a crotchety old man, would only exchange the lira back to dollars at 60 percent of the rate he'd given me just hours ago. I knew I was getting ripped off and was livid. I went to the local police station to file a complaint and found a Turkish American who offered to help me get it all straightened out.

As we were talking, the police chief overheard us discussing transporting the bus by train and told us that we wouldn't be allowed to do that. Even after showing him all my papers, he continued to tell me that it would not be permitted. Finally, he gave up arguing with me and Hassan and after some searching, we found a place where I exchanged the lira for dollars at a terrible rate. By this time my patience was wearing thin when Hassan then told me that his brother was the ticket agent and he could convince him to sell me the tickets today. This helped my attitude; I just wanted to buy the tickets and get everything ready for our trip the next day. We raced back to the ticket station and arrived fifteen minutes before it was due to close, but Hassan's brother had already gone home. I was exhausted, worried, and frustrated and just wanted to get back to the bus to pack and get some sleep.

The next morning, we arrived at the train station at 6:30 and tried to buy our tickets, but were run through every hurdle imaginable. They tried to separate Shelagh and me two times and both times a Turk made an unwanted advance on her. Luckily, Shelagh was of Norwegian American stock and very capable of taking care of herself, but it still scared her and really upset me. We scrambled back and forth to get papers for the bus, then I had to scramble to find tie-down ropes. It seemed they did everything they could to make this difficult, and everyone kept telling us that the Russians would not let me bring a car into the USSR.

Finally, just before losing all hope that we would actually make it, we pulled out of the Kars station with our bus on the flatbed train car. We found our seats in the old-fashioned European passenger compartment, sharing the space with two grouchy old women, a man who looked like he had just escaped from prison, and a little kid who was the Turkish version of Dennis the Menace. It took us two hours to travel the fifteen miles to the border town of Akyaka, a settlement that looked like something out of *Dr. Zhivago*, with mud huts plunked down on a wide-open, barren landscape.

At Akyaka, they took me inside the train station and while I was dealing with a bunch of paperwork, I looked out the window and saw that the train was gone! This startled me but they reassured me that the train didn't leave, they were just switching cars around. I then saw Shelagh standing at the train door looking very panicked; she had no idea what was happening. I yelled, "No sweat!" which about broke her up. She later told me she thought the train with me on board was heading for Russia without her or our VW. She was really scared!

Once the switching was done, the train finally moved forward and crossed the border into the USSR. The scenery was very grim and reminded me of something out of Nazi Germany with barbed wire–covered fences and concrete guard towers. We hadn't been traveling for very long when two guards toting AK-47s and a Russian officer who looked like he'd walked straight out of Hollywood casting came into our compartment.

USSR guard tower

The officer was pretty scary-looking with his cigarette held between his thumb and index finger and his suspicious stares aimed directly at us. He took our passports and returned twenty minutes later with two more armed guards and a man who said he was with the KGB. He told us that we would not be allowed to continue into the country with the VW bus. There was no arguing with this guy; he didn't care about what our paperwork said. A few minutes later another more official-looking older man came in.

He spoke beautiful English and to my great relief, he told us he was from Intourist, the travel agency for foreign tourists traveling in Russia. He confirmed that we would not be allowed to continue into the country with the VW bus. I pleaded and pointed again to our papers. He said that he would do his best to help us, but even though we had all the necessary papers, the Soviet Embassy had made a mistake. There was no agreement between the Turks and Russians for crossing their border. I asked him if there was any way for us to go, and he left the compartment without answering, returning a few minutes later. He said he would take a chance and let us go to the next town and we could drive from there. It took us thirty minutes to get to the next town.

Once there they told us it was forbidden to drive from there and even if it were allowed, there was no way to remove the VW from the flatbed train car. They didn't have a Russian flatbed car available to transfer our bus and transport it to Tbilisi. To make matters worse, the tracks in Russia were much wider than the Turkish tracks so we couldn't even tow the flatcar with the bus on it. I could see the tracks were at least a foot wider and that it was indeed impossible. I was devastated!

They ended up turning the whole train around, taking Shelagh, me, and our VW bus back the same long, cold, and miserable five hours to Kars. Once we finally arrived there, we were able to get into our bus, start the engine, crank up the heater, and spend the night in our own bunks. We were so exhausted and miserable that we went to bed at midnight without even eating.

You might think that the end of this story has us changing our plans and never visiting the Soviet Union, but you'd be wrong. Surely you know me by now! Yes, we were discouraged and frustrated, but I was not ready to give up on my dream to ski and visit the Soviet Union and Shelagh felt the same way. As you may recall, I'd had many experiences of continuing to pursue my dreams despite encountering obstacles.

So, we went back through Turkey to the Soviet Embassy in Ankara and got new visas and car papers that would allow us to enter through Romania into the USSR. On a side note, it took forty years for me to discover the reason they denied us entry through Turkey. My wife and I were serving an LDS (Mormon) mission in Russia and were told that foreigners—especially Americans—were forbidden to drive in that part of the USSR because of the chemical and biological warfare plants in that area of the Soviet Union.

When we returned to Istanbul on our way to Romania and the USSR, I met someone who said he could get me ten times the going rate of dollars for rubles, an exchange that I knew was crooked. At this time, I felt very upset with the Soviet government and was worried about my finances for the trip, so I agreed and followed him down dark alleys until we reached what looked like a black-market office. By this time, I was scared to death!

I handed my hundred dollars to another scary-looking Turk sitting behind a desk, and when he reached into a drawer, I was worried he was going to pull out a gun. To my relief, he produced a big bag of Russian rubles and we made the exchange. It was a frightening encounter and I was so glad I had sent Shelagh to the US Consulate to wait for me there. I learned a valuable lesson from this experience: no amount of money or revenge is worth putting yourself in danger.

We were running out of time if we were going to reach Moscow to witness the big May Day military parade in Red Square, and skiing was looking very unlikely so we drove straight through to Albiţa, Romania, a town that borders the USSR. We spent over two hours at the border as the Soviet guards ransacked our bus and went through all our personal items. They searched every square inch of the VW looking for anything they thought we might be hiding. In all my travels, including in South America, I've never been so thoroughly searched. Luckily, I had hidden the illegal Russian rubles in the walls of the VW. Another lesson learned!

We arrived in Odessa at 6:00 p.m. and as required, we met with a representative from Intourist. He told us that we were required to stay in Intourist hotels while in the USSR and could not camp in our VW bus. I was really upset and again worried about finances but at least I had made a great deal getting the ten-for-one rubles. I figured that I'd gotten the last laugh on the Soviets! Wrong. It turned out that all Intourist hotel rooms had to be paid for in US dollars. I was so incensed and Shelagh had quite a job trying to calm me down as I stomped up to our room to keep from saying something that might get me thrown into a Soviet jail.

My anger lessened a little when I saw how nice the room was; it even had a sink. After settling in, we decided to go shopping to spend some of the rubles we couldn't use for the hotel room, and to our dismay, we found the only clothes, toys, or anything worth buying were in Intourist stores, and—you guessed it—you had to pay with Western currency! In the local markets, food was scarce, expensive, and of very poor quality (except for ice cream, for some odd reason) but you could find good foreign food in the Intourist stores if you had US dollars.

Our inability to use the rubles created another big problem to solve. We didn't have much US currency left so we couldn't afford to stay in the USSR for the whole three weeks as originally planned. Reluctantly, we cut our stay to thirteen days, which meant we wouldn't have time to go skiing in Russia. I felt so bugged and upset. Not only would I miss out on skiing the Caucasus Mountains, I would have to figure out how to get all the rubles cashed back into dollars.

I tried to focus on the positive; I kept telling myself that at least the rooms were nice and they included breakfast and a city tour with a guide. It turns out that I spoke to myself too soon because when we reached Moscow we discovered that we were in the poorest Intourist hotel in the city and our room was dismal, as was the included breakfast. I continued to worry about our finances and still felt bugged and angry with the Soviet government.

They really were our enemy here, in Vietnam, and throughout the whole world, I thought. Despite my annoyance with the government, we found the Russian people we talked to very interested in America and Americans, and they tried when they could to be helpful. This was especially the case with the Intourist people who often worked hard to go the extra mile despite the government doing everything they could to prevent that from happening. Most of the Russians we met, including the military guys, were proud of their Russian heritage but hated the USSR's communist government. Of course, they didn't dare say anything negative about the government to anyone or they would disappear.

Our problems continued as we tried everything we could to exchange our rubles back to dollars in Moscow. We talked to many foreigners, but only a couple of them helped, and they happened to be the ones that Shelagh dealt with. Seems the pretty-blond-woman effect worked better than my boyish charm, and she managed to get a few dollars and German marks. We went to all the big hotels, the US Embassy, the American Express office, and finally in desperation, to the Director of the Bank of Foreign Currency for the USSR.

After telling him our long, sad story, he looked everything over and asked me if I could put all this down in writing and sign it. I did as I was told, after which he gave the paperwork to his secretary and had her make a copy of it. Next, we were sent to another secretary who eyed us suspiciously before making some telephone calls and flipping through a huge book, finally returning to the director's office. I was terrified she had found something wrong and was discussing it with the director, but to my extreme relief she returned, did some more checking, and handed me $383.50 in US dollars.

Shelagh was so nervous and upset that she almost fainted and it started to sink into my brain that if they found out what I'd done before we left Russia, they would send me to a Siberian gulag! I tried to explain to Shelagh that if they thought anything was wrong, they wouldn't have given me the US dollars and that they couldn't possibly get our exchange records from three different locations until after the four-day holiday and we would be out of the USSR by then.

After dealing with the bank and feeling like we'd finally beat the Soviets at something, we felt like celebrating. We got all dressed up for our big night in Moscow, which included dinner at the Metropol and a performance of *The Marriage of Figaro* at the Bolshoi Theatre. We looked pretty stylish, especially Shelagh in her fancy cocktail dress, but to our dismay we realized that no one dresses up in Moscow, not even for an opera at the Bolshoi.

Shelagh and I at the Bolshoi Theater

The next morning, we were excited to go to the Communist May Day military parade, but it was becoming almost impossible to get around all the crowds and checkpoints. After walking for an hour and passing twelve police checkpoints, we reached the final one. I've never seen so many armed military men and police in one place. At exactly ten o'clock in the morning, Russia's Premier Leonid Brezhnev gave a speech and the parade began. As luck would have it, this was the first May Day parade they held with no military marching and no tanks, planes, or nuclear missiles. We were so disappointed!

Years later I learned that the Soviets and Mao's Chinese were involved in an undeclared war that year—the Sino-Soviet border war—and some top Soviet military leaders were pushing Brezhnev to use nuclear weapons against the Chinese, so he was trying to deescalate the situation. He canceled all military shows of force for that year's May Day parade.

We had no idea we could have been in the middle of a nuclear war with China. Despite missing out on the military marching, we still enjoyed watching the May Day festivities. There were lots of anti-American banners, flags, and signs, but most were about Vietnam. There were also a few posters declaring how bad capitalism is, so all in all it was a little scary to be there. Still, it was fascinating and exciting, and we were both glad we went.

Moscow May Day parade

After a long and exhausting May Day, we began planning our departure. That night I learned about an American student in Moscow who had recently been arrested for stealing a small Russian bear statue from his hotel room and was sentenced to twenty years of hard labor in Siberia. All I kept thinking about were those rubles and how dumb I'd been and I knew we had to get out of the USSR before the holiday ended.

We woke at 3:30 a.m. and after packing with lightning speed, we got in the VW and headed for the Finnish border. We drove straight through, only stopping for gas. Shelagh made lunch while I drove, and I slept while she drove. Gas stations in the USSR were few and far between and as luck would have it, we ran out of gas a couple miles from Novgorod, about three-quarters of the way to the Finnish border. We couldn't find an open gas station because of the holiday but finally, with the help of a young boy, we found a woman who sold me ten liters of gas she kept in her house. I raced back to the bus, dumped the gas in, and we took off again. The boy wouldn't take anything for his help, and again I realized that I loved the Russian people but not the Communist government. Most Russians we met had been nice and helpful.

Back on the road, we'd gone only a mile or two before the VW started losing power and billowing smoke. That's when I realized that the gas must have been bad. We spent the next three days sweating bullets as we went through a very scary and difficult time trying to get a tow to Leningrad and then on to Finland.

If it hadn't been for several very helpful and caring Russians, including multiple policemen, two truck drivers, and a Finnish tour bus driver, I'm convinced I would have died of worry or ended up in a gulag. I credit Shelagh with convincing most of these people to give us a hand. She was charming and lovely and people just wanted to help her out.

We finally reached the border Sunday afternoon and because we were being towed by a Finnish bus full of tourists, the border search I was dreading was much shorter and less thorough than I thought possible. To my shock and joy, we were finally safe in Finland! I took the bus into the VW shop and they discovered the number one piston had developed a large hole right in the middle and destroyed the cylinder, head, and bearings.

Of course, they told me the warranty would not cover the repairs until I explained to them that when I bought the VW, I was told the warranty would be good even after the stated 10,000 km. (The mileage was up to 19,500.) They made some calls to Helsinki and finally agreed to cover the repairs after all. Just another example of my belief that if you don't ask, the answer is always no and to never give up. It never hurts to try, and you would be surprised at how things work out!

Over the next six weeks we traveled through all of Scandinavia, Denmark, Belgium, West and East Germany, and then into Berlin. We loved Berlin and boldly went right up to the Berlin Wall to take photos until an American military guard yelled at us to get away. "They *will* shoot you! They've shot a lot of people since putting up the wall a few years ago."

Shelagh climbing the Berlin Wall

We left and crossed into East Berlin, which was like night and day compared to West Berlin. It still looked like it did right after World War II ended; all the buildings were still torn up or blown away. There were virtually no cars or trucks and everywhere we turned there were East German guards carrying AK-47s. They were not the least bit friendly, and we felt we needed to get out of there before we got shot.

We quickly returned to the west side of Berlin and felt so much safer, then drove back to our home base in Munich and Garmisch,

Germany. My travels with Shelagh had come to an end and it was time to say goodbye to the best travel buddy I'd ever had. When I look back now, I realize that I did a lot of dangerous things and I feel angry at myself for putting Shelagh into some of those situations. It was irresponsible and selfish, and the only defense I have is that I was young and did not use the good judgment or common sense God had given me. Shelagh, if you're reading this, call me so I can apologize.

I believe that while I was ignoring God's promptings back then, He had a guardian angel watching out for us (especially for Shelagh!) while I was busy performing some of my immature and reckless antics. So, remember that it's a great thing to take advantage of opportunities, to take those leaps of faith, and be adventuresome, but as you're doing so, make sure you aren't putting yourself and others in danger or breaking the law. I was lucky, but you might not be, and I assure you I did learn my lesson!

After the USSR adventure, I spent the next three months traveling through England, Scotland, Ireland, and more of southern Europe and getting prepared for the next major part of my BHAG—to drive throughout all of Africa. I found a VW mechanic who I thought would be perfect as a travel companion, so I invited him and his friend to join me.

I set out with excitement and anticipation of a great trip, including a stop in Spain to see the running of the bulls in Pamplona, but soon I realized my new companions weren't much fun to travel with since both were alcoholics and completely unreliable. It's always a gamble when choosing people to travel with, and I was lucky I'd taken the trial trip to Spain with them to see if they would be acceptable companions for the huge Africa trip. They weren't. I thought I'd learned the dos and don'ts of picking travel companions, but it's always risky.

After my experience traveling with Shelagh, I looked for people who were good skiers and enjoyed the same way of traveling that I did. I had been spoiled with my two South America companions, Jim and Ross, and especially Shelagh. The three people I traveled through Great Britain with were terrific as well but weren't interested in traveling to Africa. After realizing that I didn't want to drive through Africa with the mechanic and his friend, I found myself without anyone suitable to travel with. I made the difficult decision to head home and earn more money so I could travel a little more comfortably, find more suitable travel companions, and be home for Christmas.

Despite the difficulties I encountered in the USSR, I never lost my love of travel, and this trip and my South America adventure kept the pilot light burning for my desire to see as much of the world as possible. There will always be highs and lows in anything you do in life, and I try to focus on and remember the positives rather than dwell on the negatives. But I always remembered the lessons I learned from those negative experiences.

OOPS!

No matter where I was traveling since I'd begun my great adventure, I always took some time to write letters to friends and family. It was my way of keeping them posted on where I was and what I was up to, plus I loved hearing back from them. One of the people I wrote to regularly was my best friend, Stuart. I met him when I was running the ski lodge and he eventually ended up working for me at Aero Wash. Stuart had joined the Navy and was working as a medic in Vietnam. He had hoped to avoid being sent to Vietnam and later joked that not only did they send him there, but they didn't give him a gun and instead splashed a big red cross on his back, making him an even more obvious target. (Stuart was always a comedian.)

While I was in Moscow, I sent him a letter detailing my next adventure and when he wrote back, he basically asked me if I had lost my mind.

"David, do you have any idea what you did to me?" he asked. "Didn't you realize that we were over here fighting the communists and Russians and that maybe it wasn't a good idea to send me a letter postmarked from Moscow?"

It turns out that when roll call came up and the commander announced that Stuart had gotten a letter from Russia, the whole group turned on him, accusing him of collaborating with the communists!

Sometimes the best intentions can have unexpected results.

BHAG GENERATOR

There will always be obstacles in your way as you pursue your dreams and goals. It can be very frustrating, but you can't let it stop you. While I was in Russia, there were many times when I was angry, frustrated, and downtrodden. I could have thrown in the towel and headed home, but I never gave up trying. My experience trying to get to Tbilisi was discouraging, but I never regretted my persistence. Sure, it could have turned out so much better, but I still believed that it didn't hurt to ask or to keep trying.

Think about a time that you overcame a nearly insurmountable obstacle to get what you wanted. Write it down, and then write about what would have happened if you had given up. What would you have lost?

6

TAKING OFF

Once I arrived back in the States, I picked up my VW bus and began the long drive home to California. I'd put aside enough money to ship the bus from France to New York and had left my Africa-equipped camper van back in Europe intending to use it in the future when I continued my world travels. I was happy to be going home for Christmas; I missed my family and my friends. I couldn't wait to show everyone my collection of neat souvenirs and was looking forward to giving everyone a memento of my trip.

Much to my annoyance, someone had broken into the van while it was in transport and stolen all my treasures! They even took some of my undeveloped film, and that hurt like heck. All these years later I still think about the photographs that I took and never got to see. As I began my drive home, I was fuming mad, but eventually, I put the anger aside and tried to remember all the good times. As I've mentioned, there will always be highs and lows when you're chasing adventure, and it does you no good to dwell on the negative. I shook it off and started thinking about what my next step would be.

Once home I started looking for the perfect high-paying job, and while searching, I made some money doing odd jobs for my stepdad Ken at the Fairmont School. There was always plenty to do at the school and I kept busy doing some maintenance work, including washing the school buses. I wanted to start flying again and Ken said I would need to wash his plane, pay for gas, and cover some minor maintenance costs if I wanted to use it. I did not enjoy these tasks.

Pressure washing the school buses was easy, but washing the airplane came with its own set of challenges and it was hard work. You couldn't just pull a hose out and drag it to an airplane that was parked nowhere near a water source. The plane had to be untied and taxied to a wash rack, where you'd have to clean grime, oil deposits, and lots of other junk from the top, the belly, and the wings. Different soaps were used for different areas of the plane, and I would have to haul all the equipment—including a ladder—out there each time I washed it.

It took three and a half hours to move the plane to the washing rack, scrub, rinse, and dry the outside, then vacuum and clean the inside and cockpit, before finally moving it back. "This stinks," I thought. I tried to find someone else I could pay to do it, but the cost was sky-high since they'd have to go through all the same time-consuming steps. Then my mind started churning. I thought about how much easier it was to clean the buses using the power washer.

You press a button and it sprays out soap, followed by a stream of water under high pressure, blasting off not only the soap and grime but also the stuck-on bugs. I started thinking about how using a pressure washer to clean the airplane would not only be so much easier, it would save a lot of time. If I could figure out a way to get water out to the plane, I could also eliminate the need to taxi the plane around to the washing rack. That would also be a big liability release.

I drew up a plan and went out to Fullerton Airport where Ken kept his plane to talk to the airport manager. He immediately dismissed the idea telling me it was too dangerous, it wouldn't work, blah blah. Not the type to be easily discouraged, I brought the idea to the Orange County airport, the Chino airport, and a few others. They all said the same thing: "Absolutely not."

I was a little dismayed by everyone's negativity, especially because no one ever gave me a really good reason why they said no. I think that sometimes it's just easier for people to say no, and that's where persistence pays off. If you keep pestering someone and they can't come up with a good reason to say no, they'll sometimes go ahead and say yes!

In my case, I believed that it was a great idea, and I wasn't ready to give up on it. Now here comes the part where "it never hurts to ask" comes in. I went to Mr. Ritchie, my former boss at the Fullerton airport, and told him my idea, even though the manager had already declined. He loved it! He agreed to have a word on my behalf with the airport manager, who was a good friend of his. Finally, the airport manager agreed to give me a shot, so I bought a used pickup truck, a water tank, soaps, and a pressure washer. I was in business!

My first Aero Wash truck

I started washing the planes Mr. Ritchie used for his flight school, and word began spreading. I also used some of the skills I'd learned managing the ski lodge, posting flyers advertising how much cheaper and safer it was to use my services. Everything was going pretty well until some bozo called the EPA to express his concern about the environmental impact my soap was having. I ended up having to buy special biodegradable soaps, which cost more money and didn't clean as well, but at least I was doing my part to save the environment, right? Eventually, I found better acceptable chemicals that worked much better.

Since Fullerton was a pretty small airport, and airplanes didn't need to be washed that frequently, I needed to figure out a way to get more business. Orange County Airport had already said no, but after Mr. Ritchie, the airport manager, and some of my customers spoke to them on my behalf, they agreed to let me work there. I eventually rented some office space at OC Airport, purchased another truck and equipment, and named my business Aero Wash Company.

It was a lot of hard work, but I was making good money and ended up buying another Corvette. I guess I never stopped to ask myself what I was doing spending money on a fast car when I was supposed to be saving up to resume my trip around the world. Maybe I figured I could sell the car to pay for my travels like I'd done before.

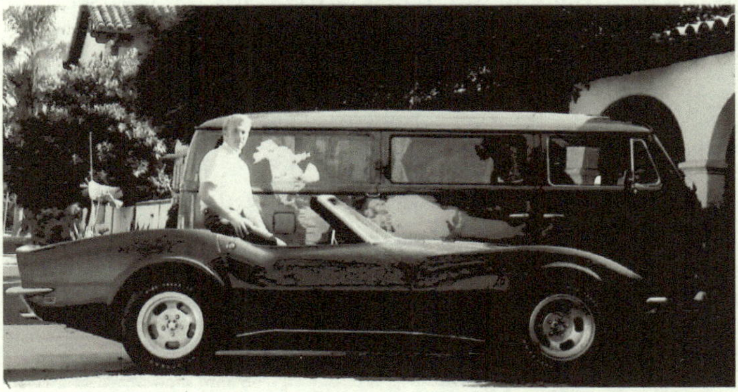

My second Corvette and travel bus

Either way, I was enjoying being a business owner and was able to satisfy my urge to fly since Ken allowed me to use his airplane to get to some job sites, with me paying all the expenses of course. It made for a pretty nice commute! Things were going so well that I started thinking I might need to delay my original plan another year. I could save plenty of money and travel without worrying about finances so much. I struggled a little when I thought about how much fun traveling was compared to washing airplanes.

The work was brutally hard since the planes were parked on tarmac that would absorb the California sun and make you feel like you were working in a pizza oven. I had to be careful not to get too sunburned or collapse from heatstroke, but luckily, I was young and fit. A surprise bonus was that the girls loved my tan and sun-bleached blond hair. I decided not to dwell on how hard the work was; I was committed to making Aero Wash a success no matter how difficult it was.

I continued growing the business and got the idea that I could service the planes at larger airports like Los Angeles International. That didn't work out because they already had it set up for the planes to be washed in their maintenance areas. Not to be discouraged, I decided that I would approach some of the fifteen airports in the Southern California area and over time was successful in getting permission to wash at all but LAX.

It was great to be working at so many different airports, so I decided to look into the possibility of getting a contract with the Marine Corps. I would watch as military fighters and transports flew into Marine Corps Air Station El Toro near OC Airport. It was a huge base that handled fighter jets and transport aircraft—including helicopters—and I thought it would be awesome to be able to work on these beautiful aircraft.

Somehow, I got approval to go onto the base and while I was there, I saw a bunch of Marines washing an F-4 Phantom. There had to be ten or twelve of them washing one airplane. "Woah," I thought. "You've got to be kidding! Why so many people to wash just one airplane?" They had an unusual work ethic, because one or two would wash while the others watched then they would switch out, with one or two washing while the rest watched. To make matters worse, I noticed they were spraying aviation fuel on the plane to help loosen some of the hydraulic fluid and grime. This was extremely dangerous since avgas is highly explosive.

I brought the matter up to a Marine colonel I knew through the LDS Church, and he arranged for me to go out to the base and talk to the admiral in charge. I told him what I'd seen and told him about my aircraft washing business, pointing out that I could do it a lot cheaper and certainly a lot safer. He liked the idea, but since it was the military, I was required to put together a bid for the work. I found out that there were several other companies doing work for the military that I'd be bidding against, so I did my greatest calculations and put in a starting bid of twenty-nine dollars for the F-4, A-4, and A-6 jets. I knew I wouldn't be making much money at that rate, but I desperately wanted to work on military planes and helicopters and knew I could grow from there.

I ended up winning the contract and actually did better financially than I originally thought I would. The twenty-nine-dollar-per-plane fee we charged was good for a year, after which time I could adjust the price and do better. The military was happy with my work, and I was successful in winning a new contract for all the aircraft at the base except the huge transport planes.

Washing an A-6 fighter jet

During the time I was working with the military, I started dreaming again about my fighter pilot BHAG. I asked a few of the pilots if they would take me up for a spin and was greeted with laughter and a big no. They said they'd end up in the brig if they took a civilian for a joy ride. "Well," I thought, "it doesn't hurt to ask!"

As always, I was keeping my ears open for more opportunities and soon heard about a military contract coming up at Norton Air Force Base (about thirty minutes from El Toro) to wash all their aircraft including the giant transport planes. Surprisingly, I got the contract, but that meant I had to buy a cherry picker truck with a basket and arm to reach the high tails and tops of these enormous planes.

My first cherry picker truck

It wasn't cheap, but I was committed and went ahead and did what I thought was a great job. I had to hire a much larger crew since we were required to wash and even do paint stripping on all their aircraft twenty-four hours a day, seven days a week. Soon we ran into a big problem: the inspectors refused to issue a pass on many of our jobs no matter how clean the plane was. With every thumbs-down from the inspectors, my frustration kept building. What was going on here?!

I spoke with one of the inspectors and was stunned when he boldly announced that he received the "gift" of a new car every year from the contractors. Clearly, he was expecting "gifts" from me too. I was shocked, confused, and angry, so I contacted the guy who'd had the previous contract at Norton AFB and even though I'd outbid him for the contract, he agreed to meet with me. It turned out that for years these inspectors received huge financial gifts from the contractors—including cars! Without these "gifts," it was almost impossible to get the washes approved or passed. This was illegal, corrupt, and immoral.

I went to the commanding general and told him what was going on, something I would later regret because I started receiving threats from other contractors. I spoke again with the previous contractor and let him know that I'd documented all this and knew some Air Force personnel who would corroborate what was going on. I threatened to go to the base commander and the FBI if it didn't stop and if my employees or I received any more threats. With the help of the general, it worked out and I kept the contract for a few years, although the inspections were never easy and always nerve-racking. This was how I learned about corruption in the government and the military.

Now that I knew how to wash huge military transports, I figured why not go after the airlines, even though they obviously had something going to keep their fleets clean. I contacted Air California, offering to wash their airliners at Orange County Airport in Newport Beach. Because the wealthy residents in the area didn't like the noise, the airport closed down at 10:00 p.m., allowing us to do the jobs on the graveyard shift.

I was successful and Aero Wash was now operating twenty-four hours a day, seven days a week in multiple areas. By this time my primary job was managing the operation and not washing airplanes myself. We were making good money, but the workload was tremendous and growing. We'd even gotten a contract with Hughes Airwest despite a chorus of naysayers reminding me that Hughes would never sign a contract with my company. I knew the chances of them agreeing to let us wash their planes was a long shot, but I took it anyway and got the contract! Again, it never hurts to try and the answer to an unasked question will always be no.

As the business grew bigger, so did the opportunity for problems to arise. Too often, I'd crawl into bed late at night after an exhausting day's work and the phone would ring. One night I got a call from the very upset CEO of Air California telling me that my crew had damaged one of their 737 airliners at Orange County Airport. They'd been forced to ground the airliner, resulting in them having to cancel a scheduled flight for the next morning and fly out a new plane and repair the damaged one at OC Airport. "What are you going to do about it?" he asked. I told him I was on my way out the door, then quickly got dressed and drove to the airport.

When I arrived, I found out that the cherry picker operator made a wrong move and punched a large hole in the horizontal stabilizer (tail). I could see there was nothing anyone could do to quickly repair it and I was sick with guilt. I called the CEO back and told him that indeed the flight would have to be canceled and asked if I could fly up to Sacramento to meet with him and show him what we would do to make sure it never happens again. He was still seething and told me to forget it, adding that he intended to cancel our contract. I pleaded with him to give me another chance, but his mind was made up.

I prayed about this, reminded myself never to give up, and put together a plan with my key airline manager. I then flew up to Sacramento to try to meet with him. Even though I was pretty certain he would refuse to see me, I felt I had to try. I'd always had a good relationship with his secretary, so she took pity on me and led me into his office. Boy, was he angry at both his secretary and at me, but then he softened and said that since I'd taken the time to fly up, he would listen to my plan.

After I apologized and showed him what I would do to avoid a repeat of what had happened, he relented and didn't cancel our contract. We paid for the damages and put safeguards in place to almost guarantee this could not happen again. The cost didn't impact us as much as it could have if we hadn't been insured by Lloyd's of London. Lloyd's was expensive but definitely worth it.

As time went on, I was able to find a few night managers to oversee the swing and graveyard shifts for the military and airline contracts and that allowed me to take advantage of another opportunity presented to me. A businessman/inventor I had met liked the way I sold for Aero Wash so much that he asked me to become a partner in his very impressive solar-powered waste-burning toilet business. I'd also be selling PolyJon outhouses for the entire US market. Since Aero Wash was thriving and wasn't as busy during the day as it was at night, I accepted his offer.

I ended up doing so well that he made me president of the National Environmental Distribution Company (NEDCO) a year later. It generated more income for me and gave me a way to travel with my family, something I loved to do. The job came with the bonus of allowing me to legally write off many of the travel costs as business expenses. I had a great time traveling for NEDCO; I would haul the outhouses all over the country to deliver and promote the "burning toilets that worked with the PolyJon outhouses." My wife, Stacey, and our three young boys occasionally traveled with me and we even got to visit with her family in South Dakota. The job was fun and lucrative, plus it satisfied my travel itch.

Soon, another business opportunity developed when my brother Bob and I concocted the idea of buying a couple of motor homes and renting them out. We also figured we could use them to travel around the country with our families, sometimes even towing a trailer with PolyJons to deliver them, and then write off the trip.

Working vacation

It was hard work and the business ended up being more aggravation than it was worth, so after just a couple of years we sold the motor homes. I was OK with the motor home rental business not working out. It was a dream, but not a BHAG and I felt that the experience taught me a lot about making sure to pick the right business. Sometimes problems with a business can reduce profits, but I loved the challenge and always learned from my mistakes.

I was happy that all the effort I'd put into Aero Wash had paid off, even though there were struggles and unforeseen incidents (like a worker punching a hole in a jetliner!). I learned how to overcome and correct the mistakes, but not without a lot of pain, sacrifice, and hard work. I had plans to expand further, in both private and commercial locations, and never let go of my goal of snagging larger military contracts, both in California and beyond.

So, despite having to put my BHAG of driving around the world on hold, I decided that I would continue to grow Aero Wash to the point where I made enough money to travel, then either close it or sell it so I could go back and finish my adventure. Read on to find out what I decided to do!

MOTOR HOME RENTAL WOES

When you run a business renting motor homes, there is an endless supply of problems to solve, repairs to be made, and demanding customers to appease. I expected issues with cantankerous generators or clogged toilets, but I never imagined how one customer would take stupidity to a new level. I'd gotten a call from a client who said he was bringing the RV back because the toilet wouldn't dump properly and an auxiliary generator was malfunctioning.

As I was standing in front of our home waiting for him, I spotted him coming up the street driving one of our twenty-eight-foot RVs. He started pulling to the curb in front of our car, but to my horror, he turned in too early and scraped the whole side of the motor home across our car. I couldn't believe what this idiot was doing!

As a result, I not only had to repair the issues in the motor home and do the normal cleaning and maintenance to get it roadworthy as soon as possible, but I also had to get my own car repaired and take the motor home to get repaired as well. Even though I always tried to keep a positive attitude, I learned very quickly that in business, you have to expect the unexpected.

BHAG GENERATOR

In this chapter, I talked about the benefits of hard work. Most of the time, hard work pays off, but you must be willing to accept that sometimes no matter how hard you try, you might fail. And that's OK.

Write a few sentences about something you dream of doing and what kind of work would be involved in achieving that dream. Ask yourself how hard you are willing to work to achieve the dream.

Work on your confidence in yourself and your team, so that when you get the opportunity, you can take the leap of faith and buy a truck or specialized equipment and put it all together. For me, it was a little scary, but it worked.

If you try something and it fails, figure out what you could have done differently or what you will do next time to make it more likely to succeed.

Finally, be prepared to eliminate or stop pursuing dreams if you realize they are not really what you want or if they are not a good fit for you or your family.

7

SHE SAID YES!

All the hard work I'd done to start up Aero Wash had paid off, and the company's success was extraordinary. Aero Wash was supposed to be a short-term way for me to earn money to continue my trip around the world, but it grew so fast and consumed so much of my time that I had to put my dreams of traveling aside. I couldn't just walk away from a growing business. I was making money and having a pretty good time working, but I hadn't completely forgotten my dream of visiting Africa, the Middle East, Asia, Australia, and the islands of the Pacific. I even yearned to return to South America. Because of Aero Wash's success, my original plan to make some quick money and continue my travels didn't work out, but that didn't mean that I'd failed in my BHAG.

As things turned out, it would just take me a few extra years (actually, a few extra decades!) to accomplish that goal. I realized that although my journey through Europe and the Soviet Union was phenomenal and I wanted to continue traveling, it made sense to save up more money and put more emphasis on finding compatible travel companions. I was still only twenty-six years old and since I wasn't considering getting married and starting a family at the time, I was happy with my decision to wait. As I look back, I realize that God knew what I wanted at that time and what was best for me even if I didn't.

My life went in a different direction when I met two aircraft salesmen, John and George. We hit it off and had a great time dancing and meeting girls in Newport Beach. For several months it was fun and exciting and I didn't think much about traveling. I was in my mid-twenties, I had a successful business and a Corvette, so life should have been great. But it wasn't. Although I was grateful for Aero Wash's success and was dating a lot of cute girls, many of them were divorcees with children and I wasn't ready for that kind of responsibility. I felt something was missing in my life, but wasn't quite sure what it was.

Then John, who was an LDS member, announced that he was getting married. I'd met his future wife and spent time with the two of them, always being fascinated by their relationship. She was an extraordinary woman and I loved the way she interacted with John and the way they treated each other. I think the universe was hinting to me that I was ready to settle down and start a family because a little voice inside my head kept telling me that this was the kind of relationship I wanted, this is the kind of woman I'd like to spend my life with. I was happy for them and looked forward to their wedding. Since John and I had become best friends, I assumed he'd ask me to be his best man but he didn't. In fact, he didn't mention my attending their wedding at all.

Finally, I brought it up to him and he told me that I couldn't go to their wedding because they were getting married in the LDS Los Angeles Temple. I was still clueless as to why I couldn't attend.

No, I wasn't an active Mormon, but I wanted to go to the wedding. I asked him what I would need to do to be allowed to attend. He told me to speak to my bishop, but at the time I didn't know who or what a bishop was. Eventually, I found out who he was and met with him. He told me that if I worked hard, I might be ready to go to the temple in six months, but more likely it would take a year. This got me seriously thinking about where I was in my life and I came to the realization that even though I was a successful businessman, I wasn't happy. Maybe it was time to settle down and find someone like John's fiancée. I had to figure out what I would need to do to find a remarkable woman like her to marry and start a family with. I came from a family of five and realized that I enjoyed being part of a large family and I wanted to have lots of kids.

John and his fiancée would occasionally talk about their Mormon faith, and I learned that it was more family oriented than I'd realized. I had attended BYU and talked to missionaries in South America and other Latter-day Saints and found myself very comfortable with the church. As I stated earlier, I found myself in agreement with much of its doctrine, so that aspect of it intrigued me, but I wasn't ready to look into it in earnest until now.

I went back to talk with Bishop Haymond and shared my desire to meet the kind of woman John had married. He told me that if I wanted to meet that kind of woman, I first had to be the kind of man who deserved somebody like that. He encouraged me to start going to church and attending church functions rather than looking for a life partner at bars and clubs. The atmosphere at church functions was much different, he said, and I would be surrounded by people who had desires similar to what I had.

These talks got me pumped up and excited, so I immediately set about trying to figure out the best way to learn more about the church.

I didn't attend church on Sundays at first but instead, I enrolled at the LDS Institute at Santa Ana College. The Institute offered religion and marriage classes equivalent to those given at BYU. I'd never taken any of those kinds of classes while at BYU, although I did take required courses about the Book of Mormon.

At that time, I was busy skiing and managing the Chateau, so I'd never paid much attention to the class. Now I felt ready and my interest was piqued, so I dove into the LDS Institute classes. It would turn out to be the best decision I ever made because it led me to become an active member of the LDS Church and meet my beautiful future companion and wife.

Everyone at the LDS Institute welcomed me with open arms. I was amazed by how friendly the girls were (not to mention gorgeous) and I immediately felt like I belonged there. There was a group of patriotic singers called the Grand Land Singers and they encouraged me to join. I had always loved to sing but had never done anything like this, and I had a ball singing with them locally. I was taking some Institute classes and learning more about the church while still getting in lots of skiing and it was a fantastic time. I felt like I fit in so perfectly that I decided to just enjoy it.

Most of the people I met at the Institute had similar moral values to what I had. I wasn't a saint, don't get me wrong, and I dated a lot of girls, but as I said in chapter 5, I believed in the Mormon tenet of no sex outside of marriage and their "Word of Wisdom" stance of no alcohol, tobacco, or coffee. I was great with all these doctrines and found myself falling in love with the Mormon Church. And then something happened that changed the entire trajectory of my life. I met Stacey.

I was out on a date with a casual girlfriend and we were sitting together on an overstuffed couch at the Institute of Religion building talking about a class we'd just taken on the New Testament. The Institute was housed in a former residence that had been built in the early 1900s and later converted for use by the LDS Church at Santa Ana College. The bedrooms had been changed into classrooms, but they kept the beautiful mahogany-paneled walls and nine-foot ceilings, giving it a turn-of-the-century-English-estate feel and charm. What used to be a magnificent kitchen was now used by students and teachers for eating breakfast, lunch, and snacks while socializing with their friends and fellow teachers.

While I was talking to my date, my eyes were drawn to the water cooler in the kitchen where I noticed a stunning young girl. I couldn't look away; it was as if my gaze was pulled by a giant magnet. I couldn't avoid the beautiful sight my eyes were beholding! At first, I thought she must be a young movie starlet, but that made no sense. Why would a starlet be at the Santa Ana LDS Institute building? I couldn't believe what I was seeing.

This girl was drop-dead gorgeous. Her hair was the color of dark, shiny amber with curls that framed a breathtaking face, showing off piercing eyes that made me feel as if I was witnessing the most beautiful sunset ever. (I know this sounds like a passage from a romance novel, but I truly did feel this way. I was smitten!) She was certainly one of God's greatest creations, sculpted to be worshipped by man!

Stacey Bryan, my future bride

All of a sudden, I became extremely thirsty. My mouth was as dry as though I had just crossed the Sahara Desert and I desperately needed a glass of water from that water cooler. (Yeah, it sounds corny, but it's the truth.) I asked my date if she was thirsty, but I'm pretty sure I didn't pay attention to her answer. I was going to get that drink of water and couldn't think of anything else. I had to meet this starlet, this model of perfection before hordes of other eager suitors circled her like hungry vultures!

As I approached the water cooler, trying to camouflage my real intentions, I could see she was trying to look like she wasn't watching me. However, it was clear that she was trying to sneak quick peeks at me. I looked around to survey the competition, hoping it was me her beautiful eyes were aimed at. Could it be that this woman of my dreams was even remotely interested in me? What do I say to her? How should I act?

"Would you like some water? It's cool and good," I said with all the class and sophistication of a slug.

"Boy was that lame," I thought, as soon as the words left my lips. Luckily, she seemed to take pity on this ancient twenty-six-year-old who longed for the courage of a lion. But what did I have to lose? So, I jumped right in like a tiger chasing its prey. "Would you like to go out sometime, like maybe tomorrow?" I nearly pleaded.

I was shocked when she accepted my bold invitation. Did she seem reluctant or was she just curious, I wondered. I couldn't believe it! I actually had a date with Wonder Woman (this is what the kids at church would call her a few years later). For those who don't know, Wonder Woman was a character from a television series in the 1970s. She was known for her great beauty, strength, and integrity.

In my head, I immediately started planning what we would do on our date. We would go out for dinner, and I would take her flying around the area. Or maybe I would fly her to Las Vegas or Santa Monica for dinner and a show. I wanted to impress her without going overboard. As I stood by the water cooler talking to Stacey, I felt like we were the only people in the room. Suddenly, I remembered I had left my date sitting on the couch. I quickly turned around to go back to her and felt terrible when I saw that she had left. I'm not proud to admit that the only thing that came to my mind was that I hoped Stacey hadn't noticed what I had done. I didn't want her to think I was a jerk. Even though I felt bad, I also realized how lucky I was that Stacey had stopped at the water cooler. I had a date with the most beautiful girl I had ever met!

I would later find out that Stacey and her aunt, who was only six months older and more like a friend than an aunt, had seen my

Corvette parked by the Institute building. They had made a bet with each other about who could get a date with the owner of the "Vette." I knew there was a reason I loved that car so much. It was a confidence maker for me, and a great icebreaker when girls saw me with it.

That first date with Stacey on April 21, 1971 was fantastic, and I felt like the luckiest man in the world. Yes, things were certainly falling into place. Stacey was everything anyone could ever have dreamed of in a girl and like me, she was still at the stage of investigating what the LDS Church was all about and learning every day. I was becoming more deeply involved in the church and soon I was ordained as an elder, which gave me the power to baptize others. After dating Stacey for a few months, she asked me to baptize her, which I proudly did.

Our courtship went pretty well, but I started to worry about whether she was really the one for me. She was eight years younger than I was and there were a lot of girls out there. How could I know if she was the right one? I suggested to Stacey that we date other people, but that didn't go very well and we nearly broke up over it. Then Stacey went back home to South Dakota and while she was gone, I prayed about it, and realized that this was definitely the girl I wanted to marry.

That is when I discovered that Stacey and her Aunt Linda had made the Corvette guy bet, but I was not going to let that deter me. I knew she was the girl for me and God had confirmed it, so I made a grand gesture by flying out to South Dakota to propose. Her aunt and grandmother cautioned me about her parents, and I imagined them as the husband and wife from the American Gothic painting—you know the one that has the scary-looking farm couple with the guy holding the pitchfork.

My future in-laws?

But I had to ask her father for her hand in marriage, and although it was scary, I did it and he gave me his blessing. I took her up to Lover's Lane in Rapid City and presented her with a small diamond ring. She said yes! It was the beginning of the best part of my life.

The day I proposed

Meeting Stacey and committing to marry her was also the clincher of my acceptance that I wanted to be involved in the Mormon Church and I was looking forward to marrying her in the Mormon temple. We met with Bishop Haymond and asked him if he would marry us and that's when we found out that because she hadn't been a member of the church for at least a year we couldn't marry in the temple. We both understood why, but there was nothing that could stand in my way of marrying the girl of my dreams.

We ended up having a civil ceremony in a chapel officiated by Bishop Haymond, who became a lifelong friend of the family and ski buddy. It was perfect because when the ceremony was over, we were husband and wife. Remember what I've said time and time again in this book: Don't give up on your dreams. Find a way to make them your reality. Stacey and I did, and you can too.

Bishop Haymond makes it official

The early years of our marriage were full of joy even though we didn't have a lot of money. Despite being the owner of Aero Wash, I was only into the end of the second year and didn't have that much business yet, so I didn't always give myself a salary. I had to make sure all my business expenses were covered before I paid myself. Occasionally this caused distress when we had no available cash for necessities.

We had our first child in 1973, and I can remember coming home to Stacey, who was nearly in tears saying that she didn't have any money to go shopping for food. At that time, we were giving a percentage of our income in tithing, and we just had to have faith that it would work out.

One of the first doctrines of the church we committed to God to follow was tithing. We trusted the Lord in the promise He made in Malachi 3:10: "Bring ye all the tithes into the storehouse, that there may be meat in mine house, and prove me now herewith, saith the Lord of hosts, if I will not open you the windows of heaven, and pour you out a blessing, that there shall not be room enough to receive it."

That promise was the first of many doctrines of our church that we believed in and have followed ever since. We have the strongest testimony that it works. We didn't have everything we wanted, but we always had everything we needed. We trusted God to take care of us and He never let us down.

I do not want to make this a religious and preachy book about the LDS Church, but I know I would not have been as successful in any of these opportunities without God's help. I believe the ability to reach your BHAGs and to be truly happy is greatly enhanced by bringing God into your life no matter what church or religion. If you do your very best, He will take care of the rest in the pursuit of your righteous goals.

A year after we had been married civilly on November 13, 1971, we went to the Salt Lake Temple on November 20, 1972 to be sealed by a Temple Sealer who had the authority from God to establish us as husband and wife for "all time and eternity," not just "til death do you part." It was such a special time; we were so happy and ready to welcome our first child into the world and our family. We had also made another big commitment at that time when our bishop encouraged us to attend the closest temple at least two times a month. That was a very difficult commitment to make since it was a two- to three-hour drive each way because of LA traffic. But we did it and we were rewarded in many wonderful ways.

Miraculous things began to happen because of those commitments. People I had forgotten about who owed me money would show up with cash in hand. And more remarkably, Stacey kept finding money—literally finding it. One windy day she was pushing our son down the street in a stroller and a swirl of leaves containing a twenty-dollar bill landed smack in my son's lap. Back in the 1970s, twenty dollars was a lot of money, and could buy plenty of food.

Another time our son was digging around in a sandbox and pulled out a twenty-dollar bill again! We couldn't believe our eyes, and when the next miracle happened, we knew that God was looking out for us. Stacey was walking on the beach with our son when he toddled right into the surf. The water knocked him down, but Stacey was right there to pull him out and when he was done coughing and spurting water, she looked down and noticed he was holding a twenty-dollar bill in his hand.

These little miracles were a very powerful thing for Stacey and me. We listened to the promptings from God; we prayed and paid our tithe and learned that one way or another we would be taken care of. Later, when I became a bishop myself and met with people who said that they couldn't pay their tithe, that they could barely pay their rent, I could honestly tell them that the Lord would not let them go without. I knew it was true because it had happened to me. When I shared my experiences with anyone who followed the Lord's counsel to pay their tithe, they agreed that it was indeed true. We had all learned to follow the promptings sent from God, never to panic, and never to give up on the Lord.

Stacey and I survived the challenges faced by our difference in age and upbringing, including my being a workaholic. We were committed to attending the temple, going to church every Sunday, paying our tithe, and striving to keep God's commandments. It was very hard at first, but so worth it! We also strived to honor our commitment to serve in our church. I'd become the elders' quorum secretary working with adult men for a year and then I was asked to be the youth activities chairman, responsible for the church activities of the almost 150 twelve- to eighteen-year-old youths. It was a lot of work, but I loved it.

As Stacey and I began having more children, I was still running Aero Wash, and it was growing rapidly. We expanded to more airports, and although I was able to save some time by flying between airports and military airbases, I was gone a lot. To add to the demands on my time, I was called to be a counselor in the bishopric at just 29. It involved a voluntary commitment of between twenty and thirty hours a week.

I was both shocked and honored; I couldn't believe the Lord and His leaders thought I was prepared and capable of serving in this very busy and important position in the LDS Church. I couldn't see how I could balance all this, but God prevailed and I learned how to better balance my time, multitask, and work smarter. I was ordained by a visiting Church General Authority, James E. Faust, which left me in a spiritual high and feeling closer to the Lord than I ever would have dreamed.

I couldn't understand at first but realized soon that because of this new calling and our willingness to try to keep all His commandments, the Lord was giving me more energy, time management skills, and the ability to multitask so I could accomplish what I thought was virtually impossible. I not only learned how to balance Aero Wash and my new more demanding calling, but was able to add the NEDCO operation as well.

I was very successful, but I began to see that once I was released from my bishopric calling, I felt pressure to spend more time with Aero Wash and my time with family suffered. I really wanted to spend more time with Stacey and our children. The voice in my head started getting louder and louder telling me that it was time to make a change.

ONE TOUGH LADY'S LIFE IN A LITTLE HOUSE ON THE PRAIRIE

During our lives together, Stacey and I have encountered some pretty big obstacles and at times life was hard, especially early on in our marriage. Money was tight, we drove old clunker cars, I had sold my Corvette to buy another Aero Wash truck, and we struggled every day. However, Stacey took it all in stride and amazed me with her toughness. Nothing threw her too badly and I attribute that to her upbringing.

Stacey was born and raised in a Little House on the Prairie of South Dakota, just like the one in Laura Ingalls Wilder's books and the popular television show from the 1970s and 1980s. The prairie was blisteringly cold in winter and hot as heck in the summer. From first to eighth grade she went to a one-room school with only a teacher, a potbelly stove, and an outhouse. Her family of six lived in a small house with no indoor plumbing, so during the cold winters, they would have to walk through the wind and snow to use the outhouse.

Stacey's "Little House on the Prairie"

One particularly frigid night, a blizzard was raging when Stacey, who was only four or five years old, felt nature calling. Rather than use the chamber pot, she put on her coat and made her way to the outhouse through the howling wind and blowing snow, did her business, and went back to bed. In the morning her mother looked out and saw her tiny footprints in the snow. Stacey had left the cozy comfort of her bed and walked through a blizzard because she didn't like the chamber pot! That's just one example of the kind of fortitude my beautiful wife has exhibited for her entire life.

BHAG GENERATOR

This chapter's theme is centered on listening to the promptings of God. As you continue your journey toward fulfilling your dreams and goals, take a moment to listen for a little voice in your head and let it guide you.

The voice might just be a prompting from God, and I hope you listen to it. If you don't have a good working relationship with your spiritual side, I urge you to consider thinking about the subject.

Use the space below to make notes of any thoughts that come across, intuitions you have about your journey, or messages you get from that voice or that relationship. As time goes on and you pursue your BHAGs, check back on this list and see if any of the things you wrote were on target!

8

SCHOOL SHOULD BE FUN AND CHALLENGING

Aero Wash was a strong, profitable business, but as it grew it demanded the lion's share of my time. Because many of our jobs took place in the small hours of the night when planes weren't in service, I had to be available 24/7. I would work during the daytime and not come home until after the swing shift got started, sometimes as late as 11:00 p.m. Someone would call at 1:00 in the morning to tell me that something had happened and I'd have to get up and go solve the problem. Of course, this would wake Stacey and then I'd disturb her again when I got home hours later. Then I'd have to get up at 6:00 in the morning and go back to work.

This schedule was wearing me down and as patient as Stacey was, she made it clear that she was not happy with the arrangement. I didn't have enough time to devote to my church obligations, my spirituality was dropping, and I never got to see my wife and kids. The oil crisis of 1979 was in full swing, and Stacey would sometimes spend the entire day waiting in gas lines—with our three little boys in tow—to help fill up the work trucks.

Everything seemed to be falling apart and I realized that if I didn't make some changes, I was going to lose my family. It was becoming an intolerable situation and even though I loved the company, I could feel it was time to sell. The final push came when my brother told me that he'd had a dream that I sold Aero Wash, and soon after that, two offers to buy the company seemingly came out of nowhere. I didn't need any further proof that the time had come, so I sold the business.

It was a bittersweet moment when I picked up the check from the sale of Aero Wash, but having a large sum of cash and the promise of $5,000 a month for the next five years made it more tolerable. It would be wonderful to finally be able to spend time with my family and at that point I was beginning to think about what I would do in the future. That was the sweet part. The bitter part was that Aero Wash was my baby; I'd started at nothing and built it up to be a thriving business. It gave me great feelings of success and afforded me many opportunities, including tax write-offs to fly—especially to fly into military bases. That was so cool! I'd been an entrepreneur since my days as a paperboy and knew that something would come along. Before long, I was presented with an opportunity I was not expecting and originally did not want.

The day I received the check I was in a celebratory mood, and I dropped by the Fairmont School to share the good news with my Aunt Joan, who had taken over running the school when my parents accepted a call to serve a two-year mission for our church in Peru. Of course, she was happy for me, but promptly asked me what I was going to do next. I said I didn't know but that I was going to take the time to research and find something that I would love just as I loved

Aero Wash. I wanted to be with my kids and wife and I now had the time and money to figure out what I should be doing.

She stared at me for a few seconds and then surprised me by saying, "You should run the school."

I stared right back at her, ready to start reeling off all the reasons that I wouldn't want to run Fairmont, starting with the fact that I always associated school with negativity. I spent years struggling in school because of my double vision and uncaring teachers; I spent more years working as a maintenance worker or bus driver. And then there was the low salary that I would make as school director. I had a wife and four young kids and had been making $5,000 a month. I could not afford to be paid only $1,100, although I would still receive $5,000 per month, but only for five years from the date of the sale.

Before I had a chance to respond to my aunt, she launched into a spirited sales pitch, reminding me that my oldest son was just about to enter kindergarten and that if I worked at the school, I could see him every day since he would be a Fairmont student. Then, as my other children reached school age, I could see them every day as well. She pointed out that at the end of each weekday, the school closed and everyone was gone by six o'clock. There would be no more working weekends, no more middle-of-the-night emergencies, no more 24/7 work week. She chattered on, but the sound of her voice became distant as I was overwhelmed by one of the most wonderful spiritual experiences of my life.

I suddenly knew with complete certainty that this was what I was going to do for the rest of my life. Although my aunt gave a persuasive speech, I felt as though God had stepped in right at that moment and confirmed my future for me. Remember what I told you about keeping your eyes and ears open for opportunities? They are everywhere and you never know when you're going to be presented with one. Yes, becoming comfortable in an educational setting would take some time, but I knew that it was the right thing to do for myself and my family and I knew that I would give it my all and do my best. With a helping hand from God, even a person who essentially hated school and associated it with nothing but frustration and discouragement could do a good job.

I decided right then and there to take over Fairmont Schools. My parents had asked me several times in the past if I had any interest and I'd always poo-pooed the idea. But not this time. This time I just knew it was the right path for me. Immediately, my aunt and I placed a call to my mom and Ken, who were on their mission in South America. They were super happy about it; they had been anxious to retire and go on more missions for the church. The timing couldn't have been better.

Mom and Dad's mission

Although I knew in my heart it was the right decision, I did express a few concerns to Ken about my qualifications for running a school. The only work I'd ever done at the school was janitorial and maintenance; I certainly wasn't a teacher or an administrator. He reminded me that at its core, the school was a business and that I was a successful businessman. I'd started three businesses of my own; I knew how to hire people and how to get the best from my employees.

"You can do it," he said. "Hire the best teachers and administrators, give them everything they need to be successful, and then hold their feet to the fire."

That was something I understood from my years running Aero Wash, the Chateau Après, and NEDCO. If an employee isn't cutting it, you release them and find somebody who can. Firing people is one of the worst parts of being a boss, but it's also an important policy to adhere to. Ken's words sparked my enthusiasm even further and I soon began my life in the academic world with confidence in both my ability and the knowledge that I'd made the right decision. Within a week I began working at Fairmont School as business manager and within a year I would take over as director.

Much to my surprise, I instantly fell in love with the field of education and realized the huge difference between public schools and Fairmont Private Schools. I loved working with kids and had great experiences with them through Fairmont, our church, and the Boy Scouts of America. I was impressed with the nurturing, supportive learning environment fostered by the high ideals and expectations of Fairmont's excellent teachers.

When I began my job there, I sat in on some classes and often found myself reluctant to leave, even from a particularly lively English grammar class. I, David Jackson, the kid who hated English class, the little boy who struggled so hard to learn how to read, was enjoying a grammar class! I was amazed by what I was witnessing; it was so interesting and exciting and I was overcome with the realization that school did not have to be a torturous experience; it could be fun!

I decided right then and there what my next BHAG would be: to make Fairmont School the best and most prestigious school in the world. I had a great head start in achieving this goal since Fairmont was already an incredible school, but I wanted to make it even better. I wanted to make it the best.

By now you know that I'm a firm believer in "If you don't ask, the answer is always no." With that in mind, I started visiting every school in my area—and beyond—and asked the principal or superintendent if I could sit in on a class. Most public and private school heads would tour me around the school and together we would visit classrooms, but would not allow me to sit in a classroom on my own.

I was able to visit classrooms on my own a few years later when I became part of an accreditation visiting team, which was very helpful. I saw some very inspiring teaching in both affluent and poor schools throughout the country. Unfortunately, I also saw a lot of average to poor teaching and disinterested teachers while visiting schools, especially during our accreditation visits. Nonetheless, I was almost always able to find something positive in my school visits and gain something valuable for Fairmont.

I want to share one school visit to illustrate what I have found is happening much more often than anyone realizes. I will change the names and locations to avoid hurt feelings.

I visited a public school in California that a younger friend had attended in an area we were considering as a location for a new Fairmont School. The principal, who I will call Fred, was new to the junior high school and very open and helpful as we toured. In most classrooms, I was not impressed with what I saw. Many teachers did not seem invested in what they were doing, and the students were not very involved and in some cases were unruly. I was embarrassed for the principal since it didn't seem the atmosphere changed much when we entered the classroom to observe.

We then came to another classroom and as we entered, we saw the teacher sitting and reading a newspaper, feet propped casually on his desk. As we opened the door, he peered over the newspaper at us and then to my shock, continued to read and ignored us. The students were noisy and somewhat unruly, but actually not as bad as other classrooms we had already visited. I was waiting to see what the principal was going to say to this teacher who I felt was very disrespectful of us as we entered the classroom.

When we got up to the teacher's desk he again peered over the top of the newspaper and exclaimed rather loudly, "David, what are you doing here?"

I automatically answered, "John, what are you doing?"

I felt very uncomfortable, and so did the principal as he quickly told me that we needed to leave, which we promptly did. Outside, Fred told me he didn't know what to do as John was one of his most tenured teachers and he couldn't do anything about it. I could tell he didn't want to say anything more about this so we moved on and made a couple more stops before I left.

John was a neighbor friend of mine and our wives were also friends. We knew them well and saw them often. That weekend I ran into John and could not avoid asking him what happened when we came into his classroom.

"Oh, that," he said. "That principal is new and doesn't know what he is doing! They don't give me what I need to teach and I don't get any support."

"Why don't you quit then?" I asked.

"Are you kidding? I just received my PhD in education and got a big raise. I can retire in five years with a great income!"

"But what about your students, John?"

"Oh, those brats, they don't care and don't even try anymore."

I was stunned by his words and asked, "How many of your fellow teachers feel this way?"

"You'd be surprised. A lot of them are fed up and feel the same way I do. They can't fire us—we have tenure and the Teachers Union will protect us."

Unfortunately, I have heard about and witnessed this type of teaching and met these types of teachers for years. I spent over a year trying to help back in the 1990s when then–Secretary of Education Lamar Alexander talked with me after we were awarded the prestigious Blue Ribbon School of Excellence distinction by President Bush. I felt inspired when he suggested that I join with Blue Ribbon schools in California to help other public and private schools achieve Blue Ribbon status and to support President Bush's America 2000 initiative. I could not find any organization to join that represented California's Blue Ribbon schools, so I started the California Association of Nationally Recognized Schools.

Me with the US Secretary of Education

I met with leaders of public and private Blue Ribbon schools to discover ways to help all schools strive to become Blue Ribbon schools. I was then asked by the Orange Country, California, Department of Education to be their chairman of the America 2000 committee for Orange County. I was given the authority and asked to reach out to all twenty-eight school superintendents and their principals to push the America 2000 initiative. After a couple of years, I could see that I was running into opposition from the public-school sector, who did not like being led by a private-school leader. I hated to give up, but I realized I was not making a difference in the public sector but could do so much more by channeling those efforts into Fairmont.

I continued to visit as many schools as possible well into my career, and even when Stacey and I traveled for pleasure or for the church, I made visits to schools. I soaked up every last bit of information from these visits, making note of what I thought worked and what didn't. I became adept at spotting exceptional teachers and applied what I'd learned to my own work at Fairmont. I must tell you that over the years and after interviewing hundreds of prospective teachers, I became pretty good at spotting the phenomenal ones.

When I returned to Fairmont after these school visits, I could also spot those Fairmont teachers who were my change agents. Some teachers would say, "Oh no! What is Mr. Jackson going to change now with some new idea or invention?" The change agent teachers were the ones who were excited about new ideas or inventions and would help get the rest of the faculty to embrace them.

One of my duties was to interview potential Fairmont teachers, and one of my favorite things to ask was "Think about all the teachers you've had from preschool through to college. How many were exceptional teachers who had a positive effect on your life? What made them exceptional?"

To my shock, most could think of very few teachers who had an impact on their lives, and almost all of them said that the biggest quality that made them exceptional was that they cared and were able to show it. They took a personal interest in their students, had faith in their abilities, and reminded them that they were capable. They also had high expectations of both themselves and their students. Remember what I told you about the importance of believing in yourself? That's what these educators taught their students to do.

To achieve the pinnacle of success and have Fairmont become the best and most prestigious school in the world, I set another BHAG. What if I could find, hire, support, and train enough exceptional teachers to guarantee that every Fairmont student had a great experience every year in every class from preschool through high school? That would change the world.

When I think back to my own experience, it makes me sad to think that if I'd had exceptional teachers, I might have gotten a much better education. I worked hard to ensure that no child at Fairmont Schools would ever be labeled "the dumb kid" or disregarded because they were too much trouble to help. I believe my legacy at Fairmont will be that I hired teachers who are great to exceptional and that I helped set our schools on the path to reaching the BHAG of having only extraordinary teachers. I believe Fairmont is closer than any school in the world to achieving that goal.

So, there I was, in my mid-thirties, running a private school with over five hundred students on two campuses and learning new things every day. I had a beautiful family and was committed to the church; I was beginning a great new adventure and I felt good. Of course, there were obstacles to overcome—there always are—one of which was the handful of Fairmont employees who doubted my ability to run a school.

I was the owner's son and I had no education experience, so what was I doing there? I dealt with my fair share of "Your dad wouldn't do it that way" or "Your mom isn't going to be happy with that decision."

It really peeved me, but I didn't let it affect my performance. There are always going to be naysayers in life and you have to learn to ignore them. I learned over time that confidence, persistence, and willingness to try new things were the keys to success. Follow your heart like I did and you'll do fine in the long run. It isn't always easy to ignore the negative people you encounter, but if you practice doing it, you'll get the hang of it. I wasn't born knowing how to let antagonism and disapproval slide, but I did learn. And you can too.

As I continued pursuing my BHAG of making Fairmont the best school in the country, I learned to follow my instincts and I asked a lot of questions. A favorite way of getting information was to walk around the campus and talk to the students, a habit that I continued for decades. One day when I was showing two principals around, I stopped a young lady at the high school. I asked her to tell my friends about her experience at Fairmont and she launched right into a passionate speech about how much she loved the school.

She said that everyone helped her so much that she had just been accepted into a prestigious college. She wanted to be a doctor, she said, and had accumulated enough AP credits to get her on a fast track to a top medical college. She raved about her teachers, saying that not only did they support her in the classroom, they often attended events she was participating in. I asked her to talk a little about a particular teacher who made an impact on her and was surprised when she mentioned every single teacher she'd had since preschool. She demonstrated to me that we were getting closer to my goal of providing a fantastic teacher for each year since she had been at Fairmont for fourteen years.

It was one of the best interviews I ever had with a student and the two principals with me were blown away (their words). In fact, one of them asked if I had set the interview up! I was so intrigued by this young woman that I looked up her records when I got back to the office. I figured she was one of those students who was born brilliant, and I was shocked to discover that when she was in the early grades, she did very poorly and ranked in the sixtieth or seventieth percentile nationally, which is not good at all.

However, I noticed that all of her teachers had praised her on report cards and each year she got better and better. By seventh grade, she was getting all As and Bs, and her teachers praised her hard work and mentioned how proud they were of her. Her teachers cared enough about her to push her and assure her that she could do it. They continually encouraged her and told her how proud they were of her. I tell you this story of an average girl who turned into a superstar so you will see that positivity, perseverance, and hard work pays off.

We have stayed in touch since she graduated from Fairmont and approved using her name in her story. This former struggling Fairmont student, whose name is Rani Berry, never gave up and ended up fulfilling her dream of becoming a doctor. She graduated medical school early and eventually took a position as a gastroenterologist at Stanford Health Care. I sometimes wonder what I could have accomplished if I had the same opportunities she had.

During my years at Fairmont my entrepreneurial drive, my never-give-up attitude, and my belief that if you don't ask the answer is always no helped grow the school to five campuses, each having individual personalities to serve the broadest range of students. We've won countless awards for excellence, including the prestigious National Blue Ribbon School of Excellence award from the president of the United States. We've welcomed students from all around the world and opened ten partner schools in several Asian countries.

I enjoyed a fulfilling career as the head and then owner of Fairmont Schools and I owe it all to perseverance, hard work, and the ability to trust and believe in myself. If a discouraged, underachieving boy like myself can end up running one of the most prestigious schools in the world, imagine what you can do. Identify your BHAG, make a plan, and get to work. You'll be amazed at what can happen!

PAYING IT FORWARD

Years ago, I got to know a young man named Zack, who was a member of our church and who helped me with photos and videos on my computer. We got to talking and I asked him what his hopes and dreams were for the future. He surprised me when he said that he wanted to be a doctor. Zack was very shy and lacked any confidence, so my first thought was that there was no way he should pursue a medical career. He didn't seem to have the drive to take on such a monumental task.

Then I remembered what my dad always told me: "If you really want something, and are willing to work hard and not give up, you can do anything you put your mind to."

I wanted to be like my dad, encouraging and helpful, so I talked to Zack and asked him the same question Ken always asked me when I was trying to figure things out. "OK, how badly do you want to be a doctor and what do you need to do to make this happen?"

I gave him some suggestions on how to proceed and we talked it through. To my delight, Zack had more drive and desire than I had given him credit for. With a little financial help, he went back to college with a renewed goal and belief in himself!

Eventually, he was accepted to a medical school and was on his way to fulfilling his dream. We stayed in touch and I continued to encourage him, and he surprised everyone when he graduated from medical school and announced that he'd be doing his residency at a hospital starting in 2024. We also witnessed his new belief in himself as we attended his marriage to a beautiful LDS girl in the LDS Temple. I am so proud of him! I was pleased with myself for not being a naysayer when he told me his BHAG. Instead, I paid Ken's great advice forward and reminded Zack not to give up on his dreams, especially when he knew they were right for him and his new wife.

BHAG GENERATOR

In this chapter, I've shown you that by doing your best, never giving up, and having faith in yourself and God, you can do amazing things. I've also demonstrated that BHAGs are not a one-time thing; they can change as you make your way through life.

Think about what your present BHAG is and write it down. Compare it to the BHAG you had before you read this book. Has anything changed? Is your BHAG even bigger and hairier? I sure hope so. Don't limit your dreams; go for the big one, work hard, and believe it will happen.

9

LANDING AT THE TOP

So here I find myself starting the last chapter of this book, and I realize that I've only told you stories from the first half of my life. I was blessed to have many more adventures in the past several decades, but there's only so much room in one book. I thought about it and decided that I would use this final chapter to share with you some highlights and inspiring stories from more recent years. I guess I'll just have to write more books in the future if I want to include everything I want to say to you!

There are several areas of my life from which I've chosen a few stories to tell you about: family, church, my career in education, and travel. It's my hope that you will read these stories and be inspired to embrace the principles I've been talking about throughout the book: dream big, believe in yourself, it never hurts to ask, ignore the naysayers, and take risks. Remember, without risk, there is no reward! Let's take a look at some more examples of putting these principles into action.

CHURCH: BECOMING A BISHOP

It was 1990 and my dad, Ken Holt, was serving as bishop for our ward when the devastating Bedford Canyon fire hit our rural family compound and community in Southern California.

It destroyed twelve homes including my brother Bob's and sister Rebeca's and did $250,000 of damage to our home, nearly costing us our lives. More about that in another book. The experience scared my mom so badly that she insisted they move out of the area, and that's just what they did.

Corona fire

When Ken was released from serving as bishop, I was called to fill this special position. At first, I felt overwhelmed since being a bishop would take up thirty to forty hours a week and I was already working full-time at Fairmont. I was also the president of the National Independent Private School Association and the Orange County Private School Association. Plus, I had a wife and five children who needed my attention and had a three hour round trip to comute to work at Fairmont.

I felt that my risk of failure was pretty substantial since I was already spread so thinly, but I also knew that this call came from the Lord, as our First Presidency had prayed and approved my calling. I knew that with the Lord's blessings I could handle it, and so I accepted.

David's bishopric

In the LDS Church, a bishop is the leader of up to a thousand-member congregation, much like a pastor, priest, or rabbi. The bishop is sometimes referred to as the father of the ward because he is responsible for the individual church members. He is not paid for the time he spends overseeing both the spiritual and temporal needs of the individuals in his ward. So, you see how the job can be quite time-consuming.

As is my habit, I dove right in and attacked the workload head-on. I was getting up at four o'clock in the morning and working far into the night. Stacey was understanding at first but soon started to grumble a little about the hours I was keeping. A bishop friend of mine suggested that I put Stacey in charge of my schedule, so she became my appointment secretary and was able to set up meetings in our home and at my church office, generally overseeing my timetable for the day. It also gave us more time to spend together, so it was a win/win.

I had initially worried about the effect my new position would have on the time I'd be able to spend with my children, but it turned out that I not only saw them often at Fairmont Schools, I also was spending more time with them at their weekly church activities because I was expected to attend as many as possible. I stopped worrying so much about the risk to my family and worked hard to actively help as many people as I could. And there were a lot of people seeking help! Members would come in to talk about all kinds of problems—some of them quite serious.

I counseled weekly with my families, much as a family counselor, but more spiritually guided in how to help these members of the ward, and the Lord truly guided me as a bishop. I worked harder than I have ever worked and with the Lord's help, I was more successful and felt closer to Him than I ever thought possible! It was difficult but supremely rewarding.

There's nothing like the feeling you get when a member comes to you with tears in their eyes saying, "What in the world did you say to my spouse? They're a different and happier person now!" or "Bishop, I did what you and the Lord counseled me to do, and my life is so much better for it." I take no credit for changing these people's lives. I was called by God to serve, and I feel strongly that I was an instrument in His hands.

It was very risky to take on the role as bishop, but the rewards were spectacular.

CHURCH: HUMANITARIAN MISSION IN RUSSIA

Prisons are not intended to be nice places, but in some countries, they are more dreadful than you can imagine. In 2006, Stacey and I volunteered and were called to serve in Russia on a two-year humanitarian mission. One of our projects was to provide aid to a juvenile penitentiary. We'd heard the stories about the grim conditions in Russian prisons and despite the ever-present danger of dealing with Russian governmental institutions, we went anyway.

Upon arrival, we were greeted by a warden straight out of central casting. Nasty, irritable, angry, and mean. We quickly found that because of the seventy-five years under communist rule and treachery, many Russians were distrustful of everyone, had little or no faith, and were very hard to get to know. This warden was convinced that we had an ulterior motive for visiting the penitentiary even though we assured him that we had the best intentions; we really were there to help in any way we could.

Lucky for us, the warden had been made aware that a ranking Russian government official had requested that we visit, so he reluctantly agreed to meet with us. It was a complete waste of time because the warden couldn't think of anything he wanted. I'm sure there were a hundred things he could have mentioned that would have improved the lives of the young inmates, some of whom were there for no good reason.

There was always a need for warm clothes, blankets, and food, but he insisted that he needed time to think about it and told us to come back another day. I don't know if he realized how much time it took to travel to this out-of-the-way penitentiary, but I'm pretty sure that he couldn't have cared less.

So we left and eventually returned to meet with the ungrateful, angry warden, who escorted us to the kitchen area of the prison cafeteria. He showed us around and announced that he wanted two electric hand dryers for the kitchen workers.

It took every ounce of self-restraint not to blurt out, "Are you kidding me? Hand dryers? This is what you've come up with?"

I was annoyed to think that the warden wanted something to benefit the workers rather than the prisoners. Many of them were still children and deserved something, anything! But that is what he requested, so we sent our project request to our Russian leader in Moscow, hoping it would be turned down as a ridiculous waste of time.

Ultimately it was approved, and we took on the project. Incredibly, because of the red tape involved in every aspect of government in Russia, it took us an entire year to finally supply them with the dryers. It would have taken a few days for me to find the dryers, buy them, and deliver them if I'd been allowed, but no. We had to return often, usually because of tiny errors on the forms and letters, but we had to follow the rules no matter how ridiculous they seemed to us.

One of our requirements when doing a humanitarian project is that when the goods have been delivered, we will go and meet with the recipients, talk to them, and take some pictures. This is done mostly to be sure they actually received the goods. So, after several trips over that long year to correct any errors, we finally went back to the penitentiary and were escorted into the kitchen where we were greeted by a smiling gentleman who shook my hand and posed for several pictures.

"Gee," I thought to myself. "Why couldn't we have dealt with this friendly guy in the first place instead of with the cranky warden?"

Before we left, we needed to meet with the warden one last time to request a thank you letter from him. The smiling gentleman escorted us to the warden's office and took a seat behind the warden's desk. It was only then that we realized the smiling gentleman *was* the warden!

We didn't recognize him because his demeanor was so completely different that it changed his physical appearance. Gone was the scary, angry warden, and in his place was this smiling, congenial guy. It was remarkable and Stacey and I were on the edge of our seats waiting to find out what had brought about this change.

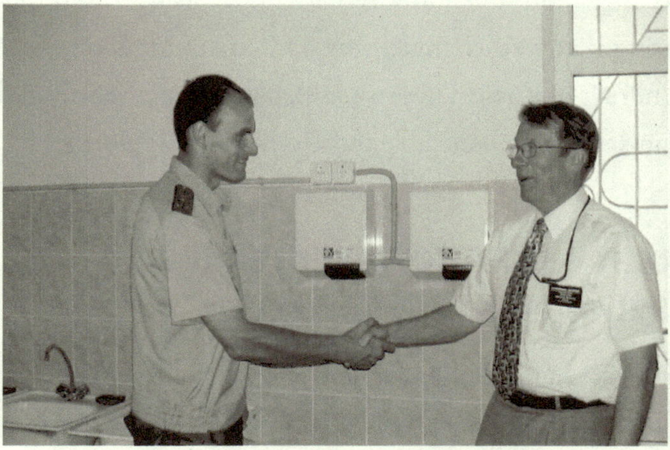

"I want to tell you something," began the warden. "I've never had anybody help me or do anything for our organization without wanting something in return. When I first met you, I was sure that you'd want something from me. But you didn't. You're the first people who've ever done something for us for no reason except that you wanted to help. I want to thank you and your church."

All three of us had tears in our eyes, and it was clear to me that this man's life was forever changed. It was one of the most rewarding experiences we'd ever had on a Russia mission. I met with the warden one last time before we left to ask him whether he could use his influence to help one of our Russian church members whose son was in prison. It was freezing and the man needed blankets and warm clothes. I'd figured that the wardens probably knew each other and felt it was worth a shot to see if our warden could help out.

He immediately turned dead serious and said that he wouldn't dare do that. He told us that if someone did anything that might make any government official (like a warden) look bad, they'd put out a contract and have that person killed. I can't say that we were surprised since we'd heard many horror stories, so we just thanked him and left.

As I said earlier, this mission was not without its risks. But the reward of knowing that we'd changed this warden's outlook on life coupled with hundreds of Russian lives we saw changed and improved through the organizations we were able to help made it all worth it.

CHURCH: A MOVING EXPERIENCE AT A RUSSIAN MENTAL FACILITY

On our Russia humanitarian mission, we worked with many hospitals, sanatoriums, orphanages, and organizations to help the blind, deaf, and invalid. One such place they call a "mental boarding school" for the mentally ill, but it is more like a hospital than a boarding facility. Earlier, we had supplied them with a refrigerator, air-conditioning, and bathroom and kitchen upgrades, but this time we went back with a group of about twenty-five Russian youths aged twelve through eighteen.

These youngsters were all church members who had never been involved in a service project before. In fact, they were completely unfamiliar with the concept of serving others; it just wasn't part of the Russian culture. We were excited to introduce them to the world of service to others, but they were understandably unsure of what to expect. We arrived at the facility on a warm summer day and since the weather was so agreeable, many of the patients were outside in the courtyard area.

After meeting with the facility's supervisor, we took the kids outside and as they approached the patients, they all froze. They didn't know what to make of this gathering of mentally ill people, some talking to themselves, others mumbling and walking around in circles, but most just sitting doing nothing. They were scared, and we weren't surprised. We were also uneasy but knew we had to show by example that there was nothing to be afraid of.

I spoke very little Russian and wasn't sure what to do, but suddenly I felt a prompting from God, and I just walked right up to the patients and started talking to them in English. None of them spoke English, but I kept talking anyway, and they started smiling and gathering around me.

Soon Stacey followed suit and began talking to other patients. She had brought along a tote bag that had photos of our grandchildren printed on it, and she showed it to the patients. They smiled and seemed to love the attention. Soon she was surrounded by patients oohing and aahing over pictures of children they didn't even know!

The kids in our group began approaching the patients when we gave them books and Stacey's bag to help—they began mimicking what we were doing and before long, they were reading to the patients and talking with them in Russian. I noticed a few people who seemed uncomfortable, so I got the bright idea to sing the only Russian song I knew to them. Before long several of the kids started singing and the courtyard turned into a joyful celebration of human connection. The transformation brought tears to all our eyes.

That night at our devotional discussion, we heard the most heart-warming testimonials from virtually every kid. This one visit changed the lives of both these mental patients and our Russian youth. This story illustrates the importance of taking risks and the astonishing rewards that can come when you do. We took a chance to bring this group of reluctant children to visit mental patients and were rewarded. The kids took a chance by approaching people they were scared of and were rewarded by witnessing the happiness they'd brought to some lonely patients and the joy they felt from doing so!

EDUCATION: THE ACADEMIC PENTATHLON

We've all heard stories of longshot successes, and they never fail to thrill and amaze us. I want to share with you one such story that is close to my heart and is one of the earliest, most exciting, and emotional moments of my career in education.

In 1989 I learned of an academic competition called the Orange County Academic Pentathlon, where seventh- and eighth-grade students compete in five subjects. Each grade had three teams that comprised A-, B-, and C-level students. I called the organizers and asked if Fairmont Schools was eligible to enter and was told that they could, but not to get my hopes up since no private school had ever placed in the top six. Private schools were much smaller than public schools, and it generally took about ten years to build team culture and gain the experience to win.

As you know by now, naysayers never get in my way, and I immediately began looking into entering Fairmont in the competition. I spoke to my junior high school teachers and managed to muster up a nine-student team and a seventh-grade teacher/coach to train them.

After practicing for a few months, the Fairmont team took part in the competition, but the results would only be revealed at an awards ceremony that neither the coach nor most of the team members wanted to attend. They knew they were a longshot to place in the top six, so most of them stayed home. Stacey and I attended and were happy to see one student and his mother in the audience. The student sat next to me and told me that he would give anything to win a medal and that he had never won anything in his life. I silently said a prayer and waited for the results to be called.

When they announced the winners for literature, his was the third name they called. He had won a medal! He jumped up from his seat, nearly hitting the ceiling, and whooped with joy. His mom had tears running down her face. We were all overcome with pride and happiness for the student and for the Fairmont team. By the end of the ceremony, he had five medals and Fairmont had picked up many more and had shocked everyone by placing second overall out of 385 schools. It was the first time a private school had ever placed in the top six, and we were ecstatic.

Academic awards

Fairmont continued to compete in the Pentathlon, and in 1992, they accomplished something that had never been done and to this day has never been repeated. They took first place in nineteen of the twenty possible team and top overall student awards and second place in the twentieth. Fairmont Schools had shown the spectacular ability of its students and teachers and proven that we were academically superior to all other schools in the county. I'm so glad I didn't let the organizers discourage me from entering our students because no private school had ever done well before. These six Fairmont students and I celebrated an impossible feat!

Unfortunately, I was not able to stop them from adjusting the rules, so no team could ever repeat our feat again. We have managed to place first in the sixth-, seventh-, and eighth-grade competitions every year for the last thirty years. It is another example of how hard work and belief in yourself (and in this case, belief in my students and teachers) can lead you to great achievements. Some would feel it might embarrass the school to enter and not win something, but the reward made the risk so worth it, especially for that one student and his mom.

EDUCATION: FOUNDING FAIRMONT HIGH SCHOOL

When I took over as director in 1980, Fairmont School was solely a kindergarten-through-eighth-grade institution with five hundred students. After about five years, Stacey and I started talking about adding a preschool to Fairmont. She was very vocal and supportive of the idea, so we went ahead and did it. To this day there are preschools on all of Fairmont's campuses and they've been very successful.

However, I've never been the kind of person who is happy just to sit back and let the good times roll, so I got it in my head that Fairmont should add a high school. Why stop at eighth grade when you can take students all the way to twelfth? However, everyone I talked to said it was a difficult thing to do, a crazy idea, and that high school is a whole different animal from a K-8 school. By now you know that skeptics have never stood in my way, so I started thinking seriously about adding a high school.

After graduating from Fairmont, about half of the students went to public high school and the other half to private schools. I can't tell you how many times our graduates would come back to me complaining about how bored they were, especially for the first two years of high school. They said that they'd already covered much of the material and were frustrated and not learning anything new.

I got so sick of hearing this that I finally went to two of the biggest Catholic high schools in the area and told them that Fairmont students needed classes that would challenge them. To their credit, the Catholic schools tried to figure out a way to create special programs to accommodate Fairmont students but ultimately decided that it wasn't possible. There just weren't enough students to justify adding special programs. I would have to come up with another plan.

The problem hit me personally because all three of my sons had graduated Fairmont and we were struggling to find high schools that suited them. We tried a local private school, which was a mistake, and finally settled on a brand-new high school that boasted hi-tech facilities and was recommended by three of our church friends who taught there. My sons loved it, but not for the right reasons. Two of them had been B students at Fairmont but now found themselves getting straight As. Their teachers loved them and complimented their fine work, so on the surface it looked like it was a good decision. And then Stacey and I went to back-to-school night.

After touring several of their classrooms and hearing their teachers rave about our sons, we ended up in the science room where the students' projects were displayed. Both boys had gotten an A, but the projects looked very familiar. It turned out that my son Dan, a senior, had turned in a project he'd done at Fairmont in eighth grade and Chad turned in a seventh-grade project for his junior project.

Neither had gotten an A for the project at Fairmont; in fact, Dan had gotten a B and Chad had received a C in middle school science! I asked them if they'd changed anything in the projects and they both said, "I changed the title and date, of course." Clearly something had to be done. The high schools were just not capable of providing a quality education for Fairmont graduates.

I immediately began researching the statistics on education in our area and was shocked to find that even some of the elite high schools had appalling rates of competency in math, English, and science. My suspicions about the state of education in California were solidified when I read Lance T. Izumi's book.[2]

Izumi found that contrary to popular belief, schools in the best neighborhoods were not the finest; in fact, their rates of college readiness were horrible, even in the most elite public schools. The California Department of Education keeps records of student achievement and college readiness, and the stats I found there were just as grim.

That was enough for me to know that my decision to start a high school was the right one despite the negative reaction I'd gotten from so many people, including my dad and my wife. Ken said that I was being foolish, that I could easily drive Fairmont into the ground financially. He was 100 percent against the idea and would not offer any financial help, so I borrowed against our house. Stacey had misgivings but extracted from me a very difficult bargain and went along with the high school expansion.

The first Fairmont High School was located on our existing Anaheim campus where we purchased and converted the building next door. Mickey Mouse from Disneyland hosted the ribbon-cutting ceremony for us.

---

2 Lance T. Izumi, (Pasadena: Pacific Research Institute, 2007), 242.

Fairmont High School Grand Opening

Soon after, I found an extraordinary facility just five minutes from Fairmont called the Philip A. Stanton Estate. It was a Spanish Colonial estate built on an acre lot in 1929 and completely renovated in the early 1980s. They'd invested over two million dollars to rebuild it and it was beautiful. In fact, it was nearly perfect.

At the time I looked at it, it was owned by the bank and was going up for auction, so I moved quickly and was able to purchase it for just under a million dollars. It only cost about $100,000 to convert it into a school since they'd already installed locker rooms and showers for the executives of the company that had been leasing it. We had our high school, and I was able to use the original high school building at the existing campus to expand our junior high program.

Over the next five years, I was able to make a deal with the owners of the properties behind the high school and to one side, expanding the size of the campus to over seven acres and buying the land at a fantastic bargain price. Although it took ten years to finally turn a profit on the high school, it was a huge success. Enrollment in Fairmont's preschool through eighth grade soared because parents loved the idea of having their children attend the same school for their entire pre-college education.

The Fairmont Preparatory Academy, as it's now called, ended up being well worth the risk. And to all the naysayers and cynics who tried to discourage me from going after the dream of having a high school, I say, "Never mind you. Without risk, there's no reward and if you dream it, you can do it."

Fairmont Prep campus

CHURCH: TEACHING SELF-RELIANCE (SR) IN RUSSIA

In 2015, we again volunteered to serve a mission for our church. They asked us to return to Russia and introduce a new program teaching self-reliance to its members. We were stationed in Moscow but our assignment was to introduce four self-reliance classes throughout all of Russia and Eastern Europe. Among other things, the self-reliance classes teach members how to handle money, how to find a job, how to find and pay for an education, and how to start a business. While we worked on translating all the books and videos into Russian, we started two groups in English in Moscow.

One group was very interested in starting and growing a business, but we worried that the program would be very difficult in Russia. There's so much red tape, bribery, and under-the-table dealings when it comes to Russian business, and we worried that the ten young people in our first group would not be successful. We were worried that if we failed, it would make both the church and us missionaries look bad.

In the end, we decided to go ahead with the classes, mostly because of the enthusiasm of the youths. They really wanted to learn so they could make their lives better. We had been promised that the self-reliance manuals were exceptional and that if the students followed the lessons exactly, they would be successful. We also shared how I'd started my own successful businesses to show them real-life examples. We took the plunge and met with them every week, and after the twelve-week course was through, we asked the young members to share their experiences with each other and to do a demonstration related to the business they wanted to start.

Self-reliance class

I was amazed at their creativity and the amount of hard work they put into the classes. Every one of them gained enough confidence to start a small business, and I found out a year later that several of their small businesses were very successful.

It was a lot of work for us and our Russian students, but we were so proud of these twenty-somethings being willing to do something that their friends and family thought impossible. Just thinking of starting a business in such a harsh environment makes me shudder. I'm so glad we took the risk of presenting those kids with what seemed like an impossible goal because in the end, it turned out to be entirely possible!

EDUCATION: THE COLLEGE PROMISE

Up until now, I've shared stories of success that came out of taking risks, but here's a story to show you that no one succeeds 100 percent of the time and to reassure you that it's OK to fail. Even if you give it your all, sometimes things don't work out, but it's not the end of the world. You just have to shake it off and move on to the next dream or goal. No one is perfect!

In chapter 8, I told you about a young girl at Fairmont who had gone from being an underachiever in our elementary school to an extraordinary high school student and later went on to become a renowned gastroenterologist at Stanford Health Care. She's the one who was gushing about every teacher she'd had from preschool to twelfth grade at Fairmont. I got to thinking about her and wanted to find out if her success was an anomaly, so I hired someone to go through six years of Fairmont records, track the kids' progress, and then find out where they'd been accepted for college.

When I got the results, I was shocked to learn that 98–100 percent of students who'd started at Fairmont in the early grades had been accepted to a top 100 college, and that includes the Ivy Leagues. What was more amazing was that one-third of those students were like Rani Berry, the Fairmont graduate who became a gastroenterologist. They started as average B/C students and by the time they graduated they were accepted by the top 100. That was an astonishing success rate and I wanted more people to see that a Fairmont education basically guarantees acceptance at the best colleges in the country. So, I came up with what many said was a hare-brained, risky, stupid idea.

I called it the Fairmont College Promise and, in a nutshell, it stated that if you start your child at Fairmont at the beginning of seventh grade or earlier and they stayed through to high school graduation, I'd guarantee that based on a sliding scale of when they started and what their GPA was first semester of their senior year, your child would be accepted into a top 100 college. They would also receive enough scholarship money to cover what parents had paid in tuition for four years of high school at Fairmont. If not, and again based on a published sliding scale chart (see enclosed), Fairmont would refund up to 100 percent of the tuition you'd paid for the four years—ninth through twelfth grades—at Fairmont.

My administrators and college counselors were opposed to this until I showed them the statistics that showed 95–98 percent of all Fairmont graduates historically were accepted at the top 100 colleges. Finally, they agreed, although reluctantly.

We appeared on ABC TV and everything was going great until the scandal involving celebrities bribing colleges to get their children admitted hit the news about a year later. Within a few weeks, we were contacted by several top 100 college admissions people advising us that because of the scandal we needed to discontinue the Fairmont College Promise; it might look like we were involved in the scandal. Our attorneys and my staff all agreed, so to my tremendous disappointment we discontinued the promise. We did honor it three and four years later for those who had signed up for it, and there was only one student we had to refund a few thousand dollars.

Fairmont Promise, ABC TV

As you see, no one succeeds every time. We spent a lot of time and money on this dream of mine, but in the end, the timing was bad, and we couldn't have seen that coming. Did that stop me from trying new things in the future? No way! You just pull yourself up by your bootstraps, chalk it up to experience, and move on.

Quartile & Years Attended Fairmont Chart

If for some reason either or both promises are not fulfilled for a student, Fairmont will contribute scholarship money to the college of his/her choice. The amount of scholarship money will be based on the quartile the student is in at the first semester of his/her senior year and the number of years the student has attended Fairmont Private Schools. The following provide examples on how to use the chart.

Example 1: If your student at graduation is in quartile one and has continuously attended Fairmont since preschool (ten years or more by the 8th grade), the promise would be the maximum of 50% for each promise to a total of 100%.

Example 2: If your student at graduation is in quartile two and has attended Fairmont for six years by the 8th grade, the percentage would be 37.5% for each promise to a total of 75% of the Fairmont tuition paid.

TOP COLLEGE PROMISE

CONSECUTIVE NUMBER OF YEARS ATTENDING FAIRMONT		PERCENTAGE BREAK
Quartile 1		
Pre-K/JK	**10 years or more**	50%
Kindergarten	**9 years**	47.5%
Grade 1	**8 years**	45%
Grades 2-5	**4-7 years**	42.5%
Grade 6	**3 years**	40%
Grade 7	**2 years**	37.5%
Quartile 2		
Grade 1	**8 years or more**	40%
Grades 2-5	**4-7 years**	37.5%
Grade 6	**3 years**	32.5%
Grade 7	**2 years**	30%
Quartile 3		
Grade 1	**8 years or more**	30%
Grades 2-5	**4-7 years**	27.5%
Grade 6	**3 years**	25%
Grade 7	**2 years**	22.5%
Quartile 4		
Grade 1	**8 years or more**	25%
Grades 2-5	**4-7 years**	20%
Grade 6	**3 years**	15%
Grade 7	**2 years**	12.5%

COLLEGE SCHOLARSHIP PROMISE

CONSECUTIVE NUMBER OF YEARS ATTENDING FAIRMONT		PERCENTAGE BREAK
Quartile 1		
Pre-K/JK	**10 years or more**	50%
Kindergarten	**9 years**	47.5%
Grade 1	**8 years**	45%
Grades 2-5	**4-7 years**	42.5%
Grade 6	**3 years**	40%
Grade 7	**2 years**	37.5%
Quartile 2		
Grade 1	**8 years or more**	40%
Grades 2-5	**4-7 years**	37.5%
Grade 6	**3 years**	32.5%
Grade 7	**2 years**	30%
Quartile 3		
Grade 1	**8 years or more**	30%
Grades 2-5	**4-7 years**	27.5%
Grade 6	**3 years**	25%
Grade 7	**2 years**	22.5%
Quartile 4		
Scholarship is not applicable. However, historically, XX% of our students do receive scholarships every year.		

REV. 07/11/17 8:38 AM

College Promise breakdown

EDUCATION: CHATTING UP JACK WELCH

Sometimes your dreams and goals are big and sometimes they're small. Sometimes you know in your heart that this or that goal is a long shot, but if you're like me, you go for it anyway. Why not? Here's a story to prove to you that it never hurts to ask and the experiences you can have in the process of trying can be almost as fun as the reward (if you get the reward, that is).

I'd always been a fan of former president and CEO of General Electric, Jack Welch. He was voted the top CEO of the twentieth century, and I was just enthralled by the guy. I'd read all of his books and knew a lot about him, including the fact that education was close to his heart. I got it in my mind that if I could just meet him, I might talk him into joining Fairmont's board of directors. Everyone said I was crazy (nothing new there), but when I found out he was going to be speaking at a conference in Las Vegas, I talked Stacey into joining me and off we went.

The event took place at a large hotel and was attended by five thousand people. I got there early so I could get a seat in the front row, knowing that after these kinds of speeches, they hold a question-and-answer session. When it was time for the Q&A, I tried desperately to get his attention until he finally called on me. I can't remember what I asked him, but I do remember that he rubbed his chin and said he was stumped. He had no answer for me and would have to think about it.

GE's CEO, Jack Welch, stumped

After the event ended, Jack left the stage through the side and in hopes that he would still be there, I walked through the curtain that led to the backstage. I was wearing a suit and tie and acting like I was someone who belonged there, so the security guards let me pass without a second glance. I found Jack talking to a few people and inched my way up to him, waiting for him to finish. I ended up more or less cornering him, at which point he said, "Hey, you're the guy that stumped me!"

I admitted that I was and then immediately launched into my pitch to him to join our board of directors. I told him about Fairmont's stellar record and offered to set up a teleconference with him for the board meetings. I just wanted him to join our board. He was silent for a second and then he handed me his assistant's business card and said, "You know, you've intrigued me. I have to go now but call my assistant in a week or two and I'll fill her in on your idea. Let me think about it. I probably won't be able to do it, but I promise I'll think about it."

I was practically giddy with delight. Jack Welch was going to think about it! Well, it ended up that he declined my offer because he was going through some personal hard times, but just the fact that he'd considered it was enough for me. Just think, if circumstances in Jack's life had been a little different at the time, there's a good chance he might have said yes. You see, anything is possible if you have confidence in yourself, push yourself a little out of your comfort zone, and ask.

On a side note to this story, several years later I got a phone call from my son Dan, who was on a private jet flying from Washington DC to Florida for business.

"Hey Dad," he said. "Guess who I'm sitting next to?"

I had no idea; it could have been anyone.

"Who?" I asked.

"Jack Welch. We're partnering with him on our executive training program."

I was thrilled and probably a little envious of Dan; I was such a big Jack Welch fan. I wish I'd had the presence of mind to have Dan ask Jack if he remembered the guy who stumped him with a question at the Las Vegas conference and then proceeded to ask him to join a board of directors for a school he'd never heard of. I like to think that he would have remembered me.

EDUCATION: SAM CALAVITTA OPENS HIS DOOR TO A STRANGER

As the director of Fairmont Schools, I was always on the lookout for outstanding teachers. I wouldn't go so far as to poach teachers from other schools, but if I heard about a particularly talented teacher, I would make it a point to approach them and let them know that if they ever wanted a change, my door was open for an interview. I kept hearing about a teacher named Sam Calavitta who worked at a Christian school in Yorba Linda. Everyone who knew him said he was fantastic, so I tried to contact him but never was able to connect. I did have his address, however, so one evening I had the crazy idea of driving to his house and knocking on his door. And that's exactly what I did.

Lucky for me, Sam answered the door and after I told him who I was, he invited me in. I was a complete stranger to him, but he was gracious and welcoming. I told him that I'd heard great things about him and launched into my spiel, telling him that Fairmont would be a great fit for him and reassuring him that I wasn't trying to steal him away from his school (although I guess I was). After our talk, I gave him my card and said if he ever wanted to change schools to contact me.

We shook hands and I left, crossing my fingers that I'd hear back from him. It took a year and a half, but I finally heard from him and was thrilled when he said he was interested in working at Fairmont. He laughed, telling me that he couldn't believe I came to his door unannounced and that my passion for Fairmont and education really impressed him and his wife.

Sam began working at Fairmont and far exceeded my expectations as a teacher. The man has an incredible gift for reaching students and was certainly born with the teaching gene. To give you an example of his skill at sparking students' interest, I want to tell you about the day when I was walking around campus and the head of our Prep High School said, "You need to see this! Dozens of students skipped lunch to watch what's going on in Mr. Calavitta's classroom and see who is winning." I went over to have a look and saw Sam standing on his desk conducting a lively calculus competition with a crowd of students yelling and cheering for the two teams vying for victory. And the most amazing thing about it was that this competition was taking place during lunchtime!

This is just one example of what makes Sam an exceptional teacher. He regularly arrived at school early and left late because he was holding competitions or helping students. That's the kind of teacher Sam is, and his dedication to the students paid off. By the third year that Sam was at Fairmont, our students did so well on the AP exams that I received a call from the College Board saying that Fairmont was not only the top performer in California or the United States but based on both the high percentage of all our high school students taking calculus and the percentage of students achieving 5s on the AP exam, we were the top school in the world!

I'm telling you this story to encourage you to go with your gut, have a little chutzpah, and take chances. (And to brag a little about Fairmont!) Yes, it was crazy to knock on this guy's door that night, but if I hadn't, Fairmont never would have reaped the benefits of this genius teacher.

FAMILY: A MOTHER AND HER SON

Family issues are unavoidable, but it doesn't always mean that there isn't love. My mom and I loved each other, our relationship was fantastic, and she and my dad were even our best friends and favorite travel companions until I took over running Fairmont. Then my relationship with my mom started to sour and was becoming tense. I confess I was beginning to avoid her at times. When I started working at Fairmont, my mom and dad were in South America on their first of three church missions and still owned the school, so I was more or less on my own.

After they returned, I didn't worry much about our working relationship because after all, they were my parents. I just assumed they wouldn't hassle me, but I was dead wrong. I learned quickly that when it came to school-related things, my mom waived the fact that she was my mother and was sometimes hard on me. It made for some uncomfortable working conditions, and the fact that she was my mother and my children's grandmother made it all the more complicated.

Frankly, she was starting to drive me crazy. She was a good woman, but she had a habit of exaggerating things to the point where she would outright lie. She would tell my sister things about me and my stepbrother and sister that weren't true and tell me lies about my sister and others. It was infuriating. It got to the point where I didn't want to be around her anymore.

Stacey took note of what was going on in my relationship with my mom and was inspired with an idea she thought might improve the situation.

"I think you should take your mom to the temple. Just the two of you," she said.

I wasn't thrilled by this suggestion at all. I did not want to drive two or three hours each way with my mom once a month. I knew it would be miserable, but I went ahead and did it anyway and guess what? I was right. She talked continuously in her usual way, exaggerating everything and saying things that just weren't true. For the first five or six months that we did this, I would spend the entire way there with my stomach churning, biting my tongue and trying to figure out how I could get through this.

The rides back weren't as bad since being in the temple has a spiritually calming effect on both of us, making us better able to tolerate each other's company. The rides there, on the other hand, continued to be nearly unbearable. It was so hard not to say something to her, not to get upset. It was a nightmare, but I hung in there for two reasons. The first was that it was Stacey's inspiration from God. The second was that I knew in my heart it was the right thing to do because she was my mother.

Then something extraordinary happened that changed my relationship with my mom forever.

Part of the temple ceremony involves what is called a witness couple. Normally the witness couple is a husband and wife, but on this particular day, the temple officiator asked my mother and me to be the witnesses. Oh horrors! I told him that this was my mom, but he said, "Is that a problem?" I'm standing there thinking, "Oh my gosh, I can't say no!" And so, my mother and I became that session's witness couple.

We sat in the front with an aisle between us, me cringing to myself and dreading the moment he called us to come forward. When the time came and they asked the witness couple to come to the altar, my mom jumped up, grabbed my hand, and led me to the altar. I could only imagine what everyone in the temple was thinking about a forty-five-year-old man being led by his mother.

I'm sure they were thinking, "Aw, isn't that cute! A boy and his mommy!" I was absolutely mortified and sat there wondering how I could possibly live through this. Finally, I said a prayer and asked God to please help me or help her or otherwise do something to change this for me. As soon as I finished the prayer, I looked across at my mother and she appeared to be aglow. Yes, it was just like a scene from a movie; a very bright light was radiating from her body.

That's when I realized that she was having the time of her life. I had no idea that sharing this spiritual experience with her son would be so meaningful to her. I decided right then and there that I had to change my attitude and figure out a way to bring her even greater joy and happiness. When we were called again to the altar, *I* was the one who jumped up, took her hand, and escorted her.

Miraculously, the rest of the session was much better, and amazingly, so was the ride home. My mom didn't exaggerate, lie, or get on my nerves the whole way back to Corona. The next day I called her, and we talked a little bit, and I believed in my heart that God had fixed her. She no longer lied; she was fantastic and even pleasant. A week or two later I called my sister Susan about this miraculous change in our mother and she seemed very doubtful.

"What are you going on about, David?" she asked. "I've spoken to Mom twice in the past two weeks and she was lying every bit as much as she always has."

I was confused. How could my sister not have noticed the difference? It was then that I realized that it wasn't my mom who had changed, it was me. Could it be that I'd become immune to all the annoying things my mom said? I know that God answered my prayer and helped me change, and maybe even helped my mom. I no longer noticed any negativity in her. The point is that from then on, we got along so much better, and that continued for the rest of her life. I had changed and recognized that when it comes to dealing with others, you have to remember that you can't change them. You can only change yourself and that can make all the difference in the world. So be yourself, believe in yourself, and trust yourself. I guarantee you'll be rewarded.

FAMILY: CORONA HOUSE FIASCO

Throughout this book, I have encouraged you to be daring, take chances, and believe that what you are doing is the right thing. I'm telling you this next story as a cautionary tale to remind you that sometimes bulldozing ahead with your plans can have negative effects on the people around you, so care must be taken not to have your head in the clouds when taking risks. Be bold, but don't be stupid.

In the early 1960s, my parents bought eighty acres of gorgeous land in Corona, California. It was their dream to have a family compound someday and be surrounded by their children and grandchildren. To that end, they offered each of their five kids five acres of land right next to the Cleveland National Forest where we could build our dream homes. The idea of living in such a beautiful area sounded really cool, and we thought it would be a great place to raise the kids, so we started making plans.

Since I'd overseen some of the expansions at Fairmont School, I decided to contract the construction of our new house myself. Big mistake! There is a reason why people specialize in different fields—most of the time they know what they're doing. I didn't. I should have just spent the money and hired a general contractor, but I like to save a buck where I can, and I figured I could handle it.

It was nearly a disaster. It was taking forever to get things done, but when I finally saw that the end was in sight, I put my house in Santa Ana on the market thinking it would take several months to sell. Of course, it sold in two weeks, leaving my family and me with nowhere but a partly finished house to live in. Certainly we could have found a rental or stayed at a hotel until the house was completed, but again, I like to save money if possible and I thought, "How bad can it be living in an almost-completed house?" I had no idea what I'd gotten my family and myself into.

At this time, we had four children under the age of seven and Stacey was in the final trimester of her pregnancy.

The major part of the construction was finished, but the downstairs wasn't done, we had no kitchen, and worst of all, no bathrooms. How bad could it be to share the outhouse with the construction workers? The water well wasn't finished either, but we moved in anyway. I thought it would be fine since the bedrooms were finished and we could work around the lack of a kitchen and use the outhouse, but I guess I didn't consider the challenges of living with four little kids in those conditions.

It's hard enough dealing with them in a house that has running water and bathrooms, but Stacey was such a competent and organized mother that I put my worries aside and we moved in.

Fast-forward three months: the water well contractor I hired turned out to be a crook, and since he was sent to prison, I had to get someone else to finish the well. Three months without water was terrible, although I did run a 1,000-foot hose from my parents' home up the hill to our house, but that was just a slight help.

Our house when we moved in

As if all the construction problems weren't enough, January 1982 was the start of one of the worst El Niños on record, bringing torrential rains to the area and a whole host of headaches for my family and me. Stacey had carefully packed and labeled all our belongings and left instructions on where they were to be stored. We were lucky to have both a basement and a huge attic, but most of the boxes were supposed to go upstairs.

However, the way the house was constructed, with an opening to the basement that you could easily access from outside, it was a lot easier to just unload everything into the basement and then deal with moving stuff to the upstairs later. It was three flights of stairs up to the attic and there was no way I was going to lug it all up there when everything would be perfectly fine in the basement. Or so I thought.

Unbeknownst to me, the contractor who insulated and waterproofed the basement did a lousy job, and it leaked like crazy. Since Stacey was in the final stages of her pregnancy and then our daughter arrived, I didn't visit the basement for a month or two. When I finally went down there, I saw to my horror that a whole bunch of Stacey's carefully packed belongings were floating in two feet of water. "Uh oh," I thought.

There was no way I was telling Stacey about the disaster in the basement. She had just given birth, was having some baby blues, and was overwhelmed by our living conditions. I pumped out the water, got a bunch of tables, and laid all the clothes and bolts of cloth out thinking they would dry, but instead, they became infested with mildew. When Stacey finally discovered my secret, it didn't go well and to this day I try not to bring it up. Suffice it to say, she was not happy about it.

In addition to the basement disaster, we were dealing with an incredible amount of mud that made the private road up to the house impassable at times. The clay would turn into this thick muck that was nearly impossible to drive or walk through, and I had to buy a four-wheel-drive Subaru so we could get in and out.

Of course, my boys thought it was hilarious as their dad tried to maneuver the car up and down the mud-covered road. Most of the time we made it, but several times I got stuck so badly that my neighbor had to come over with his giant Caterpillar D8 tractor and pull us out. Walking in the muck was a nightmare; sometimes your boots would get stuck, and you'd have to pull your foot up, leaving the boot submerged in the mud. The children couldn't walk in it on their own, so I often found myself balancing them while trying to remain standing and I confess that several times I dropped them into the mud. Being children, they handled it well, but it became a ridiculous comedy of errors and I couldn't wait for it to end.

Ultimately, we did survive and ended up with a beautiful 8,000-square-foot dream house where there was room for everyone. I'm not sure I would do it again; I'd probably rent something if I had it to do over. It was hardest on Stacey, but she was a trooper and we are still married, so it all worked out in the end. Still, I caution you to use common sense when going after your dreams and goals. Don't get tunnel vision as I did; think about the effect your actions will have on the people you love and be practical! As I've said before, I'm just an ordinary, sometimes pretty dumb man, who also makes mistakes! And boy this was a doozy!

FAMILY: FATHER-AND-SON SCUBA ADVENTURE

Children's personalities come in all shapes and sizes; some kids are carefree and adventurous, others quiet and cautious. And then there is my firstborn, David. When he was young, David had a gift for both getting into trouble and causing it. To say he was a handful would be an understatement, and his antics often had Stacey and me pulling out our hair. The doctors diagnosed him with attention-deficit/hyperactivity disorder (ADHD), and boy did that fit him.

We tried several methods to help not only David but all of our boys and girls. We tried Back in Control workshops in 1984 and 1985, workshops called Especially for Parents, which were offered by our church, and the Especially for Youth retreats that were fantastic. They all helped, but David's ADHD made life seem almost impossible at times for him and for us. He wasn't a bad kid, he was just hyperactive, mischievous, and at times reckless, although he could also amaze you with his compassion and his desire to do better. Still, he was driving us crazy, and we had to do more.

When he was fourteen, we contacted a child behavior specialist who promised she could help him, so once a week we took David on the three-hour round trip to visit the doctor in San Diego. The doctor worked with him for a while and then called us in for a meeting. She told us that David needed to spend more time with me—father/son one-on-one time without the rest of the family around.

As much as I wanted to help my son, I couldn't imagine how I was going to find the time to devote to him. I had four other children, I was running Fairmont School, I was a bishops counselor, and so much more. There are only twenty-four hours in a day, and I didn't see how I could do it. But I knew I had to find a way and my experience had already taught me that with God's help, I could and would find a way.

The doctor had suggested that our one-on-one time needed to be spent doing something I was not great at so we could learn together. I was to let David choose how he wanted to spend the time with me and to my horror he chose scuba diving! This was a disaster; I was not a water person at all and preferred dry land, ski slopes, or open skies. I had tried surfing and scuba diving before and was not successful. I also knew that you had to have a trustworthy scuba buddy if you wanted to survive, and David was the least trustworthy person I knew.

But that's what he chose, so that's what we did. Part of the scuba program required us to swim laps and several times David beat me. It was amazing to see what beating his dad at something did for his confidence and self-esteem. During one lesson, we were in a twelve-foot-deep pool at a high school and were required to sit on the bottom of the pool and purge our masks. It was not something I enjoyed doing; you had to take your mask off and let it fill with water, put it back on, and use your regulator to blow through your nose and force the water out of it.

David and I were at the bottom of the pool doing the purging when my regulator failed, and I couldn't breathe. I was on the edge of panic when David noticed me signaling for help, came right over to me, and did exactly what he'd been trained to do. He shared his regulator with me as we buddy-breathed while slowly swimming up to the surface and as far as I'm concerned, he saved my life. Everyone congratulated him for saving my life, another huge self-confidence builder for him.

This event was a turning point in our relationship and in his life; things improved from that point on. We had lots of great adventures together diving in the ocean and over in Catalina, and although we still had our struggles, Stacey and I considered it a success. Over a year later, something happened that helped to cement our close relationship. At that time, David was sixteen, still dealing with his ADHD, and remained a challenge for us.

David and Dave Jr. scuba diving

I don't remember what triggered it, but I was furious with him and grabbed him by the shoulders, pinning him against the wall to get his attention and get control. I was in shock when he screamed right in my face, "Go ahead and hit me!"

"When have I ever hit you?" I yelled back.

"Well, you wanted to!"

"Oh yes, you're right, I have really wanted to, but I didn't! You would have deserved it! Don't push my button!"

Just then he reached out and pushed the small round tie tack holding my tie in place, literally pushing my button. I lightly hit his shoulder with my fist and said, "I told you not to push my button."

He started laughing, I started laughing, and the tension broke. He hugged me and we embraced for some time, laughing, and crying. It was beautiful!

The moral of this story is that sometimes you have to push yourself past your comfort zone to be successful. In this case, I did not want to follow the doctor's suggestion, I was convinced I did not have the time, and I hated the idea of scuba diving. I didn't like the idea of risking failure in front of my son and the whole situation made me uncomfortable. But in the end, I did take the risk and did what I knew was right. I made the time to spend with David and it changed my relationship with him forever.

CONCLUSION

When I began writing this, my first book, I didn't know what to expect, and it turns out that what I wanted to accomplish was bigger than I ever thought it would be. During the writing process, I've reviewed all my old journals, reliving wonderful, challenging, and rewarding experiences. It's also been a little painful to remember the disappointing, miserable times. In the end, it was worth it, though. I've lived a good life so far and sharing my story with you has been a remarkable experience.

In preparing this conclusion, I've reviewed all my BHAGs and thought it would be fun to go through and list them with the results. Some of my BHAGs may not be so big, hairy, or audacious, but they were goals nonetheless and deserve a mention. So here we go, in no particular order:

BHAG #1: TO BECOME A SUCCESSFUL ENTREPRENEURIAL BUSINESSMAN

I did pretty well with this one, from my beginnings as a paperboy to the phenomenal success of Fairmont School, the Chateau Après Lodge, Aero Wash Co., and NEDCO.

BHAG #2: TO BECOME AN OLYMPIC SKI TEAM RACER (INSPIRED BY THE 1960 WINTER OLYMPICS AND MY STEPDAD, KEN)

Well, I might not have become a member of the Olympic team, but I got to race against Olympic silver and bronze medalists and came to the realization that giving everything else up to try to make the team was not worth it, so I'm happy with this outcome.

BHAG #3: TO BECOME A JET FIGHTER PILOT (ALSO INSPIRED BY KEN)

I consider this a success because I was able to fly most of my life and eventually fly a fighter jet over Russia. God knew that if I became a military fighter jet pilot, I would not have found the other joys in my life!

BHAG #4: TO TRAVEL THE WORLD AND LEARN ABOUT DIFFERENT PEOPLE AND THEIR CULTURES

I created a map in 1968 to travel and ski the world, and as stated in chapter 6, after my travels to South America, Europe, the USSR, and the Middle East, I put this on hold.

I had no intention of canceling—it would simply be delayed. When I reviewed my original map for inclusion in this book, I was amazed to realize that not only have I been successful in traveling to all the places I planned to visit when I made this map in 1968, I've gone to more places than I ever dreamed of. I've definitely fulfilled this goal since I've visited over 120 different countries and met an untold number of fascinating people. This BHAG is still in progress; I have no intention of stopping my travels any time soon!

BHAG #5: TO SKI IN AS MANY BEAUTIFUL PLACES IN THE WORLD AS POSSIBLE

Again, still in progress. I've skied in more places than I can count and plan to continue.

BHAG #6: TO FIND THE PERFECT WIFE AND RAISE A LARGE FAMILY (INSPIRED BY MY MOM AND STEPDAD AND OUR CHURCH)

I definitely met this goal. I have a fabulous wife, had eight terrific kids—five surviving—and thirteen wonderful grandchildren.

In addition to my BHAGs, I have always had goals, some big, some not. I always wanted to own a sports car. When I found the LDS Church, I wanted to be very involved in serving God and His children. I feel very good about what my wife and I and our kids have been able to do and will continue to do even after we leave this earthly home. And in concert with serving the Lord, it is my ongoing goal to help as many children get a better education than I got.

If you haven't realized it yet, Fairmont School is as dear to me as my family. I started there as a young man, working as a junior counselor for the summer camp, a janitor, a maintenance guy, bus driver, and an office worker. Many years later I became the director, then the owner and my passion for Fairmont has never wavered. Now that I am partially retired, I can spend my time and money continuing to help kids get a great education.

Writing this book has reminded me of how important being a family man, a church member, and an educator are to me. I feel blessed for the joy and happiness I've had in my life and I want the same for you. Find your passion and pursue it with everything you've got. I also came to a realization when I reflected on some of my BHAGs that if I had decided to drop everything else in my life to pursue my dream to make the Olympic team, I may not have had as many of the fantastic experiences that I have had.

I ended up choosing to pursue many BHAGs and not focus all my time, energy, and attention on only one BHAG or two BHAGs. You may need to make that choice also. I believe that God knew that I wanted much more than to be an Olympic team member and military fighter jet pilot and helped me see the other opportunities that would be placed before me. I took advantage of these, and I am so happy that I did.

Take a lesson from both my successes and failures, learn to take risks, work hard, believe that you can do it (because you can), don't let naysayers stop you, and remember that if you don't ask, the answer will always be NO! I promise you that if you put aside your fear of failure or rejection, and listen to the promptings you receive from God, you will achieve great things. You will be much more financially and personally successful and you and your family will have a better life. I pray that my story will resonate with each of you and wish you the best of everything.

ABOUT THE AUTHOR

Born and raised in Southern California, David R. Jackson embraced an entrepreneurial spirit from an early age. When he was twelve, he began his first paying job as a paperboy for the *Anaheim Bulletin* and throughout his teens he worked at several jobs, including as a janitor for Fairmont Schools, a gas station attendant, and an aircraft refueler. Upon graduating from high school, David's adventuresome nature took over and he embarked on his dream of traveling the Americas to ski. With two friends, he traveled down the Pan-American Highway to Chile, across the Andes to Argentina, and then to Rio de Janeiro, Brazil before heading back to California. It was this trip that ignited his passion for travel and he vowed to tour the world and ski in as many countries as possible.

Returning from this adventure to South America, David attended college at Brigham Young University for one year before being asked at age twenty to temporarily manage a ski lodge in Park City, Utah for the summer. This turned out to become a full-time position during which he was also made Vice President of the Park City Hotel Association and continued attending BYU and taking business courses for three and a half years. He left Park City three and a half years later and spent a year driving through Europe, the Middle East, the Soviet Union, and Scandinavia.

Upon returning from his travels, David started a successful aircraft-cleaning business and an RV rental company before taking over the presidency of the National Environmental Distribution Company. After selling his businesses a decade later, he became the Business Manager of Fairmont Schools and was soon promoted to Director.

A man of tremendous vision, David dove into his position at Fairmont, starting new classes and then acquiring and building new campuses. He later expanded Fairmont's reach by creating the

Fairmont International Academy. Dedicated to serving the educational community, he served with the Boy Scouts of America, the Orange County Department of Education Committee for George H.W. Bush's America 2000, and served as President of the California Association of Nationally Recognized Schools. He was instrumental in creating the Orange County Private School Association, and the National Independent Private School Association, serving as President for years in both.

A man of faith, David served the Church of Jesus Christ of Latter-day Saints (Mormon) in almost every leadership position, over a period of five decades, including serving as bishop for six years. He and his wife, Stacey, served several humanitarian missions in Russia and Eastern Europe while he continued his work at Fairmont Schools. In 2023 he sold Fairmont to the International Schools Partnership ISP while retaining ownership of all the Orange County campuses. Presently, he holds the title of Chairman of Fairmont Schools.

Now semi-retired, David and Stacey spend much of their time in philanthropic endeavors, working closely with the Orange County educational community. He and Stacey recently celebrated their fifty-second anniversary and reside in Orange County, where they enjoy visiting with their five children and thirteen grandchildren. Skiing and traveling continue to be his passion and he and Stacey vow to grow their list of over 120 countries visited so far.

DAVIDRJACKSON.COM

www.ingramcontent.com/pod-product-compliance
Lightning Source LLC
LaVergne TN
LVHW051917060926
847244LV00006B/3/J
* 9 7 8 1 6 4 2 2 5 9 3 0 8 *